BARBAROUS SOVIET RUSSIA

LECTOR HOUSE PUBLIC DOMAIN WORKS

BARBAROUS SOVIET RUSSIA

ISAAC MCBRIDE

ISBN: 978-93-5420-264-3

Published: 1920

LECTOR HOUSE LLP
E-MAIL: lectorpublishing@gmail.com

Mujiks

Pogroms

Droshkys, Dancing the Kremlin

A Samovar, Playing on his Ukraine

An Omsk

MR. AVERAGE MAN'S IMPRESSION OF THE MEANING OF CERTAIN RUSSIAN WORDS

"BARBAROUS SOVIET RUSSIA"

BY

ISAAC MCBRIDE

1920

**TO
NINA LANE MCBRIDE**

Acknowledgment is hereby made to the "Christian Science Monitor," "Universal Service" (Hearst), and "Asia Magazine" for courtesies extended, in using some of the material that appeared in those publications.

PREFACE

Of the five weeks I spent in Soviet Russia ten days were spent in Moscow and eight in Petrograd. The remainder of the time I traveled along the Western Front, from the Esthonian border to Moghilev, with leisurely stops at Pskov, Vitebsk, Polotzk, Smolensk, and numerous small towns. I tried to see as much as possible of this vast and unknown land in the short time at my disposal, and I tried especially to check up from first-hand observation some of the many things I had heard on the outside. I also tried to test the truth of what was told me in Russia itself,—to find visible evidence of the fairness of the claims made. Some popular fancies were quickly dispelled. Disproof of others came sometimes in vividly concrete fashion.

Soviet Russia is not unanimously Bolshevist, any more than the United States has ever been unanimously Democratic or Republican, or Prohibitionist. The speculators are not Bolshevist, nor are the irreconcilable bourgeoisie, nor the Monarchists, nor the Cadets nor the Menshevists, nor the Social Revolutionists and Anarchists. Nevertheless Russia stands overwhelmingly in support of the Soviet Government, just as the United States stands overwhelmingly in support of Congress and the Constitution. There are many who are opposed to Soviet rule in its present form, and this opposition is not confined to the old bourgeoisie and the anarchists. It prevails to a certain extent—variously estimated—among the peasants. But it is an opposition which ceases at the military frontier of the nation. I found many critics of Soviet rule within Soviet Russia, but they insisted that whatever changes are to be made in the government must be made without foreign interference. At present their first interest is the defence of Russian soil and the Russian state against foreign assault and foreign interference.

The peasant opposition is mainly due to the deficiencies in transportation and the shortage of manufactured articles. They blame this on the government, much as other peoples lay their troubles to "the government." The peasants are reluctant to give up their grain for paper money which is of no value to them unless it will buy shoes and cloth and salt and tools,—and of these necessities there are not enough to go round. While the blockade continued the government was striving vigorously to overcome the shortage of manufactured articles brought about by the blockade, knowing that this alone would satisfy the peasants. They claimed to have made encouraging progress, especially in the production of agricultural machinery, of which they were trying to have the largest possible supply ready by spring.

Whatever the state of mind of the peasants, they are certainly better off materially than the city workers. In all the villages I visited I found the peasants faring much better than were the Commissars in Moscow. They had plentiful supplies of good rye bread on their tables, with butter and eggs and milk, —almost unknown luxuries in the cities. Their cattle looked well fed and well cared for. It was harvest time and the farmers were gathering in their crops. They told me that the season had been exceptionally bountiful.

I learned after my return to America that there had been a great deal of agitation among the upholders of the old Russian order in this country last summer and early fall over the pogroms which were said to have been carried on by the Bolsheviki. I found nothing but cooperation and sympathy and understanding between the Russians and the Jews. There was no discrimination whatsoever, as far as I could see. Jews and Russians share alike in the councils of the Soviet Government and in the factories and workshops.

In fact I found nothing but the utmost kindness and good will towards the whole world, all through Russia. "If they will only let us alone they have nothing to fear from us, —not even propaganda," —was said to me over and over again. There were no threats made against the interventionists. The Soviet forces merely went ahead and demonstrated their strength and ability to defend themselves, and left the record of their achievements to speak for itself.

ISAAC McBRIDE.

"Kloshe Illahe,"
Bethel, Connecticut,
March, 1920.

CONTENTS

APPENDIX

LIST OF ILLUSTRATIONS

"BARBAROUS SOVIET RUSSIA"

CHAPTER I

ENTERING RED LAND

"You will never return alive. They will slaughter you. They will rob you of everything. They will take your clothes from your very back."

With stubborn conviction the dapper young Lettish gentleman spoke to me as he attempted to change my mind about going into Soviet Russia. He was attached to the Foreign Information Bureau of Latvia. He had been in Riga all through the Bolshevist régime, from November, 1918, to May, 1919, when the German army of occupation in the Baltic provinces drove them out. There was nothing he could not tell me about that régime. He was especially eager to impart his experiences to foreign journalists.

"Was it really so terrible, then?" I asked him.

"Nothing could have been worse," he repeated. "Many persons were killed by the Bolshevists—I saw them myself—but not so many as when the Germans began their slaughter. There was the Bolshevist program of nationalization. They nationalized the land. They nationalized the factories. They nationalized the banks and the large office buildings, and even the residences.

"Aristocratic women were taken from their comfortable homes and forced to wait on Bolshevist Commissars in the Soviet dining-rooms. One of our leading citizens, a man who through hard work had accumulated a great fortune, was put to work cleaning streets. His fine house with thirty or forty beautiful rooms, where he lived quite alone with his wife and servants, was taken away from him, and he was moved into a house in another part of the city on a mean street where he had never been before. His home was taken over by the 'state' and seven families of the so-called proletariat were lodged in it. One of our generals was compelled to sell newspapers on the streets. Our leading artists were forced to paint lamp posts—and the color was red. They made the university students cut ice."

"And the women—did they nationalize them?" I interrupted.

"Well, no, they didn't do that here in Riga," he said, "but that was because they were not here long enough to put it into effect. They were so busy confiscating property in the six months they held sway that they had little time for anything else. No, they didn't nationalize the women in Riga, but you will find they have done so in Moscow.

"But you must not go to Moscow," he added. "You will surely never return alive—but if you do, please come and tell me what you have seen." And mournfully he wished me a safe journey.

I returned to the Foreign Office the next day determined to get permission at once to pass through the Lettish front into Soviet Russia. It was a hot August day. Officers and attachés sat around panting, obviously bored that any one should come at this time to annoy them. Yet despite the heat, they were willing enough to argue with me when they learned that I wished to go into Soviet Russia. Like the young man I talked to before, they tried hard to dissuade me. They were full of forebodings.

"You will be robbed of the clothes on your back the minute you fall into the hands of the Bolshevists," they insisted.

"You must be crazy," said one particularly friendly officer, whose blonde hair stood straight up from his head so that he looked perpetually frightened.

"But I am an American correspondent," I repeated over and over again, not knowing what else to say.

"So that is it," said the officer, seeming to understand all at once. And shortly after that the Foreign Office at Riga decided to recommend the General Staff that I be permitted to pass the lines. But still they urged me not to go.

"You will come back naked if you come back alive," they shouted to me in parting.

I left Riga on a troop train at six o'clock in the evening of September 1, 1919, bound for Red Russia. By noon the following day we had reached a small town, where I disembarked with the soldiers. The front was fifteen versts away. There the Reds had established themselves, I was told, in old German trenches near the town of Levenhoff, 107 versts from Riga.

I carried a heavy suitcase, an overcoat and an umbrella, and the thought of trudging in the wake of the less heavily caparisoned soldiers was discouraging. I accosted a smart young officer with blonde mustaches. He listened to me with interest.

"I am an American correspondent," I said, "accredited to your headquarters."

He glanced at my papers and shrugged his shoulders with such an air of indifference that I thought he was not going to help me at all. But he told me to follow him, and a short distance up the road we came upon a peasant driving a crude hay-rick drawn by a single gaunt horse.

After a brief parley, none of which I understood, the peasant got down from his high seat, hoisted my suitcase into the vehicle, and I followed it. I sat flat on the floor with my feet braced against the sides of the springless cart, and we started jolting and bumping down the rough road which ran parallel with the tracks. The peasant sat on a board laid across the front of the rick.

We had gone only a short way when the booming of guns came from both sides of us. My driver, however, seemed unconscious of it. We went on for another five versts. The guns grew louder and I saw shrapnel shells burst uncomfortably near. They came thicker and faster.

I remembered the peace of Riga some twenty-four hours before this. I wanted to tell the driver to turn around and go back, and then I remembered that we did not speak the same language, and certainly, judging from his impassive back, we were not thinking the same thoughts. There was an instant when I stopped thinking altogether, and when I knew that I could not have opened my mouth had I tried to speak. A shell burst some forty feet away and a piece of shrapnel about the size of a grape-fruit landed on the floor of the hay-rick between my outspread legs, broke two slats on the floor of the wagon and dropped harmlessly to the ground. Then at last the driver turned around, his face white as chalk. His panic, instead of communicating itself to me, had the very opposite effect and I suddenly lost all sense of danger. With a boldness, which surprises me whenever I think of it, I shouted to him:

"For Christ's sake, go on!"

The driver obeyed reluctantly but soon turned around again.

"Go on!" I cried.

A few minutes later we approached a clump of trees under which stood a Lettish gun, surrounded by four or five officers. My driver stopped to talk to them, evidently inquiring whether it was safe to go on. One of the officers nodded, the others laughed, and one said in good English, "Everything is all right."

At four o'clock we reached the headquarters at the front. I presented my pass to the commanding officer, a stocky young fellow with humorous wrinkles around his eyes.

"You are an American," he said, observing me keenly.

"From New York," I said. "I am going to Moscow on important business for my paper." I told him more, giving most impressive details. I convinced him.

"Well," he said finally, "you will have to wait until morning. Both of us are using heavy artillery now."

I insisted. I wanted to go at once.

"Well, go then," he said with his first show of impatience. He called a lieutenant, gave him brief instructions and washed his hands of me.

Right across the neutral zone you could see the Bolshevist trenches, running at right angles to the railroad with barbed wire on each side so that a motor train couldn't rush through. "You can't go into the front line trenches," the commanding officer told me. "Nobody is allowed in there except military men, but you can go through the opening in the barbed wire and start across." That was the best I could do, so the lieutenant took me around those barbed wires and down into a ditch at the edge of the railroad and pointed to me to climb the bank. Well, I climbed up somehow, it was about twenty-five feet; and started down that track with my big suitcase and a heavy overcoat on, holding up my umbrella with a white handkerchief tied to it.

It was a very hot day and I had to walk two miles across the neutral zone — two miles right straight down the tracks. You could see the Bolshevist trenches in the distance. Pretty soon the firing started. I couldn't feel anything dropping near me, so I decided those Lettish soldiers were popping their heads out of the trenches to see this fool go across and the Bolshevists were taking pot shots at them.

The Lettish officer had told me: "If they start to fire on you, roll off down the bank and crawl back to our positions." But I would have had to roll twenty-five feet and probably crawl a mile. So I kept on. A scattering rifle fire spat out from the Red trenches and the shells screamed steadily overhead. My suitcase dragged heavily and I was uncomfortably warm, but I made good progress. I had covered about half the distance when a rifle bullet whipped by my ear. I plunged along the track with redoubled speed.

As I came within fifty yards of the barbed wire which the Russians had strung across the tracks, Red soldiers shouted up at me from their trenches and motioned for me to come down into the adjoining field where there was a gap in the wire. A few moments later I was in the first-line trench of the Red army.

I was hot and exhausted and still resentful of that shot. I spoke first: "Why did you shoot at me?" They did not understand, but one of them evidently knew I was speaking English. He called down the trench to another soldier who ran up. He was a tall young Slav, and showed white teeth in a broad smile as he greeted me in good English.

"Hello, America," he said.

"Why did you shoot at me?" I repeated indignantly.

"Oh," he made a deprecatory gesture.

"One of the comrades made a mistake," he said. "He shot at you without orders. But you also made a mistake."

"What was that?" I asked.

"You carried a white flag," he said, grinning. "It should have been red."

CHAPTER II

WITH THE RED SOLDIERS

I asked to be taken to the commanding officer and two soldiers were detailed to escort me. One of the "comrades" laid down his rifle and picking up my suitcase led the way down the trenches; the other shouldered his rifle and followed close behind me. I kept my eye on the suitcase and trudged along.

They were both very friendly, and with a great show of their English began talking to me at once.

"Do you know," said one of them, "that the dock workers are on strike in New York?" And while I was still wondering to myself how Russia, shut off from all the rest of the world, could have heard this piece of news, the other "comrade" burst out:

"Who is going to win the pennant in the National League?"

"Where do you learn these things?" I asked.

"From the bulletins," he replied briefly. I learned later that the wireless at Moscow works twenty-four hours a day, and that it grabs from the air practically all the news that is wirelessed from America to European countries. Each morning in Moscow bulletins carrying this information are printed and distributed in the industries, in the peasant villages and among soldiers.

For three versts we walked along the railroad track, and at last reached the headquarters at Levenhoff. I was taken to the commanding officer, who spoke English fairly well.

"What do you want here?" he asked looking me over keenly.

I had expected that question and had my answer ready. I knew I would have to give an explanation, but what I did not know was that I would have to give that explanation over and over again all the way from Levenhoff to Moscow.

"I came to look you over," I said. "In the world outside there are many conflicting stories about Soviet Russia and I want to see for myself what is going on here. I am not a spy. I should like to be allowed to go to Petrograd and Moscow and to travel through the country and then return to America and tell what I have seen."

RED ARMY'S INFANTRY DIVISION

Parading on the Famous Hodinskoe Polie in Moscow.

The Red officer took a long look at me and turned to a telephone. I knew just enough Russian at that time to get the drift of his conversation. He called up the Brigade headquarters and reported that an "Amerikanski" journalist had come across the lines and wanted to proceed into the country. There was much conversation while I stood waiting nervously. Presently he hung up the receiver and turning to me said, "You will have to report to the Brigade Command at Praele."

"And is there a train?" I asked when I learned that I had twenty-two more versts to go to Praele. There was not; I must drive there in a droshky. It would be ready for me in a few minutes. And the officer gave some orders. Presently the droshky arrived and a great powerful Red Guard with a rifle slung over his shoulder motioned to me to get in. He climbed in after me and we drove off.

It was early evening by now. Vast stretches of country swept away from us on either side of the road. I tried to talk to my burly guard, but his English was as meager as my Russian. Our conversation resolved itself into wild gestures and signs. The night was clear, brightly moonlit, and about nine o'clock it grew very cold. The chill crept into every crevice of my clothing and penetrated to my very bones, and I lost all interest in the country around us.

For hours we seemed to drive through the chill and dampness. I was fairly frozen when I realized that the guard suddenly took off his coat and silently offered it to me. I refused to take it, of course, thanking him — "Spasiba, Tovarishch!" I said. He chuckled at my Russian and repeated Tovarishch, the Russian word for comrade.

We reached Praele at midnight. My guard took a receipt for me from the commanding officer as though I were a bundle of clothes or a package of groceries, and returned to Levenhoff....

"What do you want here?"

I delivered my speech of explanation. The next question was welcome. "Would you like something to eat before you sleep?" I was very hungry. The officer called a soldier who went out and returned with some black bread and tea, with apple sauce. When I had finished eating, my guard took me to a large barrack room where about thirty soldiers were sleeping in their uniforms on wooden bunks built in around the walls. Several of them woke when we came in and looked me over with interest. They passed cigarettes and apples. We smoked and munched for awhile together, and presently every one settled down to sleep.

I awoke about nine the next morning. The soldiers were all up and gone. A guard came in and led me to a building across the street where three officers and two privates were breakfasting together. A pleasant-faced Russian woman presided over the stove. A place was made for me at the table and I was served with a very unsavory coffee-colored liquid, one egg, a small piece of butter, and plenty of black bread. While we ate a young Russian boy about thirteen years old played the violin, — the *Internationale*, the *Marseillaise*, and some charming folk-songs.

We returned to the barracks after breakfast and a little later the Commissar attached to brigade headquarters came in to see me. He could not speak English, so we carried on our conversation through the Commandant. First of all he asked what I wanted in Soviet Russia. I went through my patter and they left me. For half an hour I sat wondering what would happen next. Then the Commandant returned.

"We believe you are telling the truth," he said. "We are glad to have people come in from the outside to learn what we are doing and what we hope to do under Soviet rule. But some whom we have allowed to come in have gone out and told outrageous lies about our country and our people; others have come across our lines and have gone away and revealed our military positions to the enemy. We are defending ourselves and must be careful. You must pass on to the Division Command at Rejistza, thence to Army Headquarters, and finally to the High Command for investigation. After that you will be allowed to remain in Soviet Russia—or you will be deported."

That evening I was taken under guard across country to a small railway station where we caught a train which brought us to Rejistza at four o'clock in the morning. A bed was found for me in the station master's house. At eight o'clock my guard woke me and dragged me off to the Commissar and the military Commandant at Division Headquarters, turned me over to them and took a receipt for me delivered in good order.

After breakfast of black bread and tea came the question, "What do you want here?" I was told that I would have to wait till the following day for a decision on my case. Meanwhile I could walk about and see the town. The Commandant filled out a slip of paper which he told me I was to show to any one who offered to interfere with my stroll.

I found Rejistza a fair-sized town. The people were going about their business in normal fashion. They appeared to be in good health and they were all well clothed. Many of the shops were closed for lack of wares; others were open, though none seemed to have much stock. There was, however, an abundance of fruit in the stalls, and some vegetables. The streets were dirty. Carpenters were at work on some of the houses, many of which were badly out of repair.

I began looking for some one who could speak English, and soon discovered a young Russian boy who was eager to talk about his town.

"But why are your streets so dirty?" I asked him.

"Oh, Rejistza always was a dirty town, but we are cleaning it up now as fast as possible," he added with civic pride that was obviously newly acquired.

The streets were full of sturdy, well-clad soldiers moving through to the Dvinsk front where the Reds were bringing up reinforcements to stop the Polish offensive. Bands were playing and the soldiers marched by in good order, with heads erect, singing the *Internationale.*

I walked down towards the river Dvina. The sun was shining, the air crisply cold. A crowd of children came bounding out of a school-house and scampered towards a large park to enjoy their recess hour. They ran about playing games much as children in this country do. One group quickly marked out a space on the sidewalk with chalk and began skipping and hopping in and put among the chalked squares. Others played tag and still others played hiding games. They were all busy. The teachers had come out into the park with the children, and for an hour children and teachers alike played and talked together in the sunlight. Here or there sat a teacher on a park bench surrounded by a crowd of alert children who hung upon every word as she related Russian fairy tales.

And when the hour was over every one trooped back into the school-room with as much ardor as when they came out into the park. I wandered over to the river, but soon returned to the school-house. I wanted to find out what a Russian school-room was like.

I slipped in through the door and took a seat near by. No one took notice of me. The teacher continued her talking and the children listened with as much interest as they had outside when she was telling them of the wonderful deeds of the heroes of folk-lore. For an hour I sat and listened and then walked away still unnoticed. I returned through the town to the Commissar's house quite unmolested.

That day I dined with the Commissar and four or five of his staff. I had looked forward to the meal all day, and was grateful when at last we sat down to table. Cabbage soup and a small piece of fish were served to each of us. The others talked a great deal; I waited for more food, but none came, and I went to bed that night with a great gnawing inside of me.

I was awakened at four o'clock in the morning by a new guard who led me off to a train. The decision had been made, as the Commandant had promised it would be. The train was bound for Velikie Luki. The new guard and I had breakfast on board—black bread and two apples.

It was four in the afternoon when we reached our destination. A droshky carried us five versts to the headquarters of the 15th Army, where I was again delivered into the hands of a Commissar.

Wearily I repeated my lines, thinking much more about the possibility of getting a meal from this Commissar than I did about getting a pass into Moscow. I must have looked as hungry and tired as I felt, for the Commissar instead of granting the pass took me to his home, which was only a short way down the street.

His house seemed to me to be the most comfortable place I had ever seen. I was introduced to his wife, who came to meet us at the door. Two children soon appeared and then the Commissar's mother, and at once we began talking like old friends. I was taken to a cheerful room where I dusted and washed myself, and when I returned to the others the evening meal was set forth on the table. It seemed almost bountiful to me after the meager portions of cabbage soup and black bread I had been eating for the past few days. Actually it was only cabbage soup again, one fish ball for each, some kasha, black bread and tea. I ate ravenously, and I am afraid I gave my host and hostess the impression that I was a glutton.

I went to bed early that night feeling well fed for the first time in days. In the morning I set forth early for headquarters with the Commissar and there was turned over to a guard, who took me out to show me Velikie Luki.

The town was crowded with soldiers strolling idly along the streets, soldiers marching briskly to the railroad station, soldiers falling in and out of barracks, soldiers everywhere,—and singing, always singing, with bands and without, ceaselessly singing their beloved *Internationale*. The troops were moving out to the Dvinsk and Denikin fronts. The thoroughfares were crowded with civilians watching the regiments pass by—men, women, and children, shouting, waving caps and handkerchiefs, and joining in the chorus of the soldiers' song.

TROTZKY COMMISSAR OF WAR AND MARINE

I followed the marching lines to the railway station. Trains were pulling out and empty cars moving in as fast as they could be loaded. And how they were loaded! Passenger cars, box cars, flat cars, jammed with shouting, laughing soldiers, waving good-bye, joking and singing. Every inch of space carried a soldier. Platforms, steps, roofs, and even the engines were covered with scrambling, good-natured Reds. A train already filled drew in and emptied a load of men back from the front for a rest. The wounded were carried off carefully. From the end of the train a detachment of about two hundred disarmed soldiers marched up the platform under guard. These were the first prisoners I had encountered, and I was anxious to see what would be done with them. They marched away from the station and I asked my guard if we might follow them. He made no objection. The townspeople paid no attention to the prisoners. Evidently they were an accustomed sight.

They went about a mile down a long side street, parallel to the railroad, and then turned abruptly across lots and entered a large barrack. A sentry was posted outside, but after a little explanation my guard obtained permission for us to go in. The prisoners were seated on the floor, with their backs to the wall. Two soldiers brought in steaming samovars through a side door and others carried in great loaves of bread. Tea was made and handed around to the prisoners and the bread was cut in large chunks and given to them. The captives ate hungrily, their guards chatting and laughing with them. While they were still eating, two more Red soldiers entered, with bundles of printed pamphlets, which they distributed among the prisoners, who ate, drank, and read.

If there was a German soldier there, he received German literature; if a Lithuanian, he received Lithuanian literature; if he happened to be French—well, they had it in all languages. All the while they were holding the prisoners they fed them three times a day, sometimes bread and tea and sometimes cabbage soup, *and they kept them reading all the time*; when they were not reading some of the Commissars were in there talking with them, telling them about the world, and what the war was about and why they were sent there. They had the organization of it perfected to such an extent that prisoners were not there five minutes before they were eating, and they were not eating five minutes before they were reading.

Bolshevist warfare does not end with the taking of prisoners. The propaganda follows. The Soviet leaders think more of it than they do of bullets. They say it is more effective. Three times on the western front I witnessed this same scene where prisoners were brought in.

In Russia they like very much to take prisoners. The only objection is that they haven't got much food and they don't like to starve them. They told me that they would like to take a million prisoners a day, if they had plenty of food and paper. After all, the biggest war they were carrying on in Russia was a war of education. All along the battle-front you could see streamers telling the other side what the thing was about—you could read them a hundred yards away. At night they put two posts in the ground and fastened the streamer between them. In the morning, when the sun rose, there it was.

During the two days I spent in Velikie Luki, and later at many other places along the front, I sought every opportunity to study the Red army. I am not an expert and cannot report upon the technical details of military equipment. There seemed no lack of small arms or cannon. In general the soldiers were warmly clad and strongly shod. Certainly they were in good spirits. The relations between officers and men were interesting. There was no lack of discipline. Off duty all ranks mingled as comrades, men and officers joking, laughing, singing, or talking seriously together. Under orders the men obeyed promptly. I found it the same at the front, in the barracks, and at headquarters with the Commissars and highest officers. When there was no serious work to be done they associated without distinction.

Wherever I met the Red soldiers I was struck with this combination of comradeship and discipline. On more than one occasion I have gone into a commandant's office along the front, at some high command, and found him playing cards or checkers with his men. Privates and under-officers would crowd in unceremoniously and engage in voluble chatter without the slightest indication of superiority or deference to rank. Then, suddenly, perhaps a ring on the telephone, and the commander would receive a report of some development along the front. A brisk order would bring the room to attentive silence; cards and checkerboards and fiddles would be shoved aside. The men would file out to their posts. They seemed to have an instant appreciation of the distinction between comradeship in the barracks and discipline on duty.

THE RED ARMY

The ordinary Red soldier gets 400 rubles a month, with rations and clothes. Soviet officials told me that there were 2,000,000 thoroughly trained and equipped men in the fighting forces, with another million in reserve and under training. About 50,000 young officers, they said, chosen from the most capable peasants and workers, had already graduated from the officers' training schools under the Soviet Government. Thousands of others had been developed from the ranks.

It is easy for the casual observer to misjudge that subtle and all-important element known as "morale." I think that I am perhaps more than ordinarily skeptical of manifestations of patriotic fervor, knowing something of the means by which every general staff keeps up the fighting spirit of the ranks. But I retain from my contact with the Red soldiers a sense of peculiar zeal and dogged grit. Certainly they do not want to fight. They want to go home and settle down in peace. But this frankly confessed distaste for slaughter seems only to emphasize their determination to see the struggle through to the end. For all their war weariness they did not act like men driven unwillingly into battle. I tried to imagine myself enduring what many of them have endured for over five years, betrayed by their first leaders, overwhelmingly defeated by their first enemy, and still struggling on against new assaults from those they had been taught to believe were their friends and allies.

I tried to imagine what vast process of propaganda could have stimulated this unyielding endurance. Propaganda there undoubtedly was. Just as the Allied armies had their attendant organizations of welfare workers and entertainers to keep up the morale, so the Red Army was accompanied by a carefully organized system of revolutionary propaganda. I suppose the American soldier would not have fought so well had he not been constantly reminded that he was fighting to make the world safe for Democracy. The Red soldier is persuaded that he fights to keep Russia safe for the Revolution. This ideal is deeply personal. He feels it is his revolution; he feels that he accomplished it regardless of his leaders, certainly in spite of some of them; and now it is his to defend against attacks from without and within. In judging this thing I find myself turning away from generalizations and disregarding what I was told by those enthusiasts who have the Red Army in their keeping. I come back again and again to the men themselves. Before I left Russia I had seen a great many soldiers. I had lived with them, traveled with them, slept in their barracks, eaten in their mess. To the American of course, the conditions under which the European masses manage to maintain existence, even in normal times, is always a matter of surprise and wonder. The Soviet Government does everything possible for the Red Army. It is their constant thought and care. But the utmost that can be provided, even of bare subsistence, seems painfully inadequate to the westerner.

The preferential treatment of the soldiers, of which I had heard so much before I saw it and shared it, consists principally in maintaining an uninterrupted supply of black bread and tea. It may be propaganda, it may be a peculiar quality in the spiritual and physical composition of the Russian peasant. Whatever it is, I do not believe that any other European army would endure so long on a ration of black bread and tea. An occasional apple or cigarette were luxuries, all too quickly consumed and forgotten. The black bread and tea, constant and unvaried, will ever remain for me the symbol both of the efficiency of the Soviet Commissary and of the zeal of the Red soldier. Black bread and tea and song. Their love for song is amazing, — all songs, but principally the *Internationale*. They march off to the front singing, they limp back from battle singing, they sing on the trains, and in the barracks, and at mess; they sing while they are playing checkers and they sing while they are sweeping stables. They wake up at night and sing. I have heard them do it.

I was told that about seventy-five percent of the Czar's officers were in the Soviet Army. This was no sign that they were converted to communism. Their spirit remained essentially patriotic. They supported the Soviet Government, not because it was a Socialist government, but because it was *the* government. They fought to defend Russia.

It was Trotzky who insisted on allowing these old officers to come into the army. Many of the Communists thought they would betray the soldiers on the front and turn them over to the enemy. But Trotzky said it was a question of permitting the experienced officers to train the men and teach them military tactics or the Red Army would be destroyed. Trotzky had his way. At every army post, whether it was a company, a brigade, a regiment or a division, wherever there was an old army officer there was a trusted Commissar who worked in the office, and every move the old army officer made was known to the Commissar.

The following manifesto, drawn up and signed by 137 officers of the old régime, appealing to their former messmates to quit the counter-revolution and stop making war upon the Soviet Government, which the people had established and would defend against all attacks, was sent through the Denikin lines:

"Officers — Comrades:

"We address this letter to you with the intention of avoiding useless and aimless shedding of blood. We know quite well that the army of General Denikin will be crushed, as was that of Kolchak and of many others who have tried to put at their mercy a working people of many millions of men. We know equally well that truth and justice are on the side of the Red Army, and that you only remain in the ranks of the White Army through ignorance regarding the Soviet Republic and the Red Army, or because you fear for your fate in case of the latter's victory. We think it our duty above all to write you the truth about the position made for us in the Red Army. First we guarantee to you that no officers of the White Army passing over into our camp are shot. That is the order of the Supreme Revolutionary Council of War.

LENIN AND MRS. LENIN, MOSCOW, 1919

"If you come with the simple desire to lessen the sufferings of the working population, to lessen the shedding of blood, nobody will touch you. As to officers who express the desire to serve loyally in the Red Army they are received with respect and extreme courtesy. We have not to submit to any kind of outrage or humiliation. Everywhere our needs are attentively supplied. Full respect for the work of specialists of every kind is the fundamental motive of the policy of the present government and of its authorized representatives in the Red Army. Quite unlike the practice in the old army, you are not asked, 'Who are your parents?' but only one thing—'Are you loyal?' A loyal officer who is educated and who works advances rapidly on the ladder of military administration, is received everywhere with respect, attention, and kindness. Among the troops an exemplary discipline has been introduced.

"From the material point of view we could not be better treated. As for the Commissars, in the vast majority of cases we work hand in hand with them, and in case of disagreement the most highly authorized representatives of the power of the Soviets take rapidly decisive measures for getting rid of the differences. In a word, the longer we serve in the Red Army, the more we are convinced that service is not a burden to us. Many of us began to serve with a little sinking of the heart, solely to earn a living, but the longer our service has lasted the more we are convinced of the possibility of loyal and conscientious service in this army. That is why, officer comrades, we allow ourselves to call you such although we know that the word 'comrade' is considered insulting among you, because among us it indicates relations of simple cordiality and mutual respect. Without proposing that you should make any decision, we beg you to examine the question, and in your future conduct to take account of our evidence. We wish to say one thing more,—we congratulate ourselves that in fulfilling obligations loyally we are not the servants of any foreign government. We are glad to serve neither German imperialism, nor the imperialism which is Anglo-Franco-American. We do what our conscience dictates to us in the interest of millions and millions of workers, to which number the vast majority of the company of the officers belong."

CHAPTER III

ON TO MOSCOW

Before leaving Velikie Luki I wandered with my guard down a street of the town and came upon a Soviet bookstore. Inside were thousands of books and pamphlets, in what seemed to me all the languages of the world. The store was full of men and women buying these books and pamphlets. I learned that this store and many others like it had been opened almost two years before, and that knowledge of history and social conditions throughout the world was thus being brought to millions of Russians formerly held in darkness.

Later in the afternoon of that day the Commissar informed me that I was free to go on to Smolensk and that if I passed muster there I could go anywhere I desired in Russia. I was given another guard, a big fellow who had spent ten years in England and returned to Russia when the Czar was overthrown. He so much resembled the Irish labor leader, Jim Larkin, that I called him "Larkin" throughout the course of our journey together.

He had an exclamation which he used frequently when I was too pertinacious to suit him.

"God love a duck, what do you want now?" he would roar with a despairing gesture, and the tone of his voice also was despairing. It may be that he was justified in his complaint, for there was much that I wanted to know and to see.

On the last day of our journey towards Moscow he turned to me and said, "I haven't prayed for ten years or more,—not since I was down and out in Glasgow, Scotland, and wandered into a Salvation Army headquarters. Then I did go down on my knees and pray for help, but I decided since that praying wasn't my job. But God love a duck, when I get you safely into Moscow I'm going down on my knees again and thank God that this job is over and ask Him to save me from any more Americans of your kind."

But there was, after all, some excuse for my troubling him so often and so much. "Larkin" slept on every possible—and impossible—occasion, and the sound of his snores, with which I can think of nothing worthy of comparison, kept me awake, so that in self-defence I used to rouse him every time we reached a station to ask questions about where we were and why we had stopped there and what the people were doing and why they were doing it. When I had him sufficiently awake to begin to smoke I could snatch a bit of sleep for myself, for he invariably sat up until he had smoked eight or ten cigarettes, after which his snoring began again and my rest ended.

"Larkin's" real name was August Grafman, which sounded Teutonic. He was a Russian Jew, however, and a good fellow. I hope to see him again sometime, and I commend him to any other Americans who want to see for themselves what is going on in Russia at the present time. He spoke English readily and perfectly, and from him I obtained much information I might otherwise have missed. There was the time when we waited for a train at a small station in the course of our journey towards Smolensk. All at once a commotion arose on the other side of the station. Hurrying around, we saw a man running, pursued by three or four Red soldiers. Two officers coming toward the station drew their sabres and held them before the man, who stopped and his pursuers captured him. They brought him back to the station and I observed that he was a Jew. I wondered if his crime was that of his race, remembering stories of pogroms. The Jew was brought into the station and seated on a bench. Immediately the soldiers surrounded him, and one of them stood up in front of him and made a long speech. At its conclusion he sat down, and another rose and made an address. Finally a third vociferously questioned the man. At last the Jew arose, the soldiers made way for him, and he left the station. "Larkin" who had been too much interested in the proceedings to talk to me, now satisfied my curiosity.

The Jew had been caught in the act of picking the pockets of a soldier. Furthermore it was his third offence. The first man who spoke had tried to impress the Jew with the enormity of the crime of robbing a man who was on his way to defend his country. He had said, "Don't you realize that a man going out to fight carries nothing with him except what he actually needs, whether it be money or anything else, and that it is worse to rob a soldier on this account than an ordinary civilian, with a home, and all his treasures about him?" The second man had talked of the defence of the country; the soldiers were going to fight so that when the fighting ended there would be enough for every one and no need for stealing. The third had tried to obtain a promise that the man would not again steal from soldiers. He had been successful, and, "now the Jew is free," said Larkin.

"But it was his third offense," I said. "I should think they would punish him severely."

"Larkin" gave me a pitying glance. "You don't understand the Russians," he said simply. "They are kind and in their own new born freedom they want every one to be free."

At last our train arrived and we got on. To Smolensk and then to Moscow, I thought. But it was not so simple as that. Our train was going to Moghilev direct, so we had to get off again at Polotsk at nine in the evening, where we found that we were half an hour too late to catch the train for Smolensk. "Larkin" hunted around for a sleeping place for us when we learned that we would have to stay overnight in the town, and finally won the favor of the Commissar, who took us to what he called the "Trainmen's Hotel," a large building near the station. In the room into which we were ushered there were about twenty beds, the linen on which was far from clean. Two of the beds in one corner of the room were assigned to us and we lay down fully dressed. After what seemed a few minutes I was awakened by a vigorous kick, and found a huge Russian standing over me, brandishing his arms and speaking harshly and menacingly at me. I hurriedly shook "Larkin" out of his profound slumber, and at the end of a brief but spirited discussion between the two in Russian, he informed me that the man had been working all night in the railroad shop and had come in to sleep. He resented finding his bed occupied. I suspected "Larkin" of enjoying the joke on me, as I clambered out and shivered in the cold, but his enjoyment was brief, for he was almost immediately ordered out by another man who entered and claimed his bed.

The two of us wandered out forlornly into the cold foggy morning and went back to the station. The Commissar there made us comfortable in his office until daylight, when we went down the track to a water tank and had a "hobo wash" after which we ate our breakfast—one egg each, black bread and tea, in the Soviet restaurant in the station.

We had been told that we could not get a train to Smolensk before four o'clock in the afternoon, but at eleven the Commissar told us that a trainload of soldiers going to the Denikin front would be passing through at two in the afternoon and that it might be possible to arrange for our transportation on this train, if we wished it. We did wish it and at two o'clock we were in a box car full of soldiers en route to Smolensk, which we would reach at ten that night.

The soldiers sang all evening—Russian soldiers always sing, no matter how crowded, how hungry, or how weary—but one by one they dropped off to sleep, huddled up in all sorts of positions. The train jolted along, slowly, it seemed to me, and it was too dark to see anything through the window. My guard went to sleep, and I remember thinking we must be near Smolensk and that I would have to stay awake since he seemed to find his responsibilities resting lightly. The stopping of the train roused me, and thinking that we had arrived at Smolensk I shook "Larkin" who looked at his watch and exclaimed, "Why it's midnight. We must have passed Smolensk."

Surely enough, we had gone through Smolensk and were seventy five versts on the other side of it, bound for the Denikin front. I had no objections to going there eventually but I preferred to have permission first, so we hastily bundled out of the train and went into the station. "Larkin" approached the door of the Commissar's office and tried to brush past the Red Guard who sat there, and who objected to such an unceremonious entrance. After an interminable discussion— perhaps five minutes,—I said, "He wants to see your credentials. Why don't you show them to him? Do you want us both to be arrested?"

But the Red guard had lost patience by this time. A snap of his fingers brought a policeman who arrested "Larkin" and before I had finished the "I told you so," I could not restrain, I found the heavy hand of the law on my own shoulder. The two of us were marched down the street and locked in a little dark room in what was apparently the town jail.

In the two hours of solitude that followed I shared all my dismal forebodings with that unfortunate guard. We would be taken for spies and as spies we would certainly be shot. I couldn't be sorry that this penalty would be inflicted upon anyone so stupid and obstinate and generally asinine as he, but I at least wanted to get back to America and tell people how stupid a big Russian could be. There were probably some adjectives also, I am not sure that he listened. In any event I could not see the signs of contrition that might at least have lightened my apprehensions.

LENIN IN THE COURTYARD OF THE KREMLIN, MOSCOW, SUMMER OF 1919

At the end of two hours two Red soldiers opened the door of our cell and escorted us to the police station where we were taken at once before the judge, a simple, but very determined looking peasant, who examined first the Red Guard who had caused our arrest, the policeman who had arrested us, and two soldiers who had witnessed the affair.

"Larkin" in the meantime very reluctantly interpreted whatever comments and explanations I had to make. He became more and more stubborn and taciturn. The Red Guard told his story, which was verified by the policeman. The two soldiers further attested to the truth of the tale and stated that we had been entirely at fault. Then the judge asked my guard for an explanation, and with the air of one playing a forgotten ace which would take trick and game, "Larkin" produced our credentials and laid them triumphantly on the judge's desk.

When he had read them the judge rose and made a statement which I demanded my guard should translate.

"Oh he is just saying," said "Larkin," "to please tell the American that we are sorry this thing happened. We are only working people and we must be careful to guard our country. The Red Guard at the door was simply obeying orders and doing his duty, and we want the American to understand that no deliberate offence was intended. There are so many people making war on us, both inside and outside, and we have to be careful."

When "Larkin" had translated my reply, which was to the effect that we acknowledged our fault, and had only congratulations for the men who understood their duty and had the courage to perform it, and that I regretted having been the cause of so much trouble, the judge himself led us to a first-class train coach in the yards, unlocked it, and told us to enter and spend the rest of the night there.

"At eight o'clock in the morning this coach will be picked up by the train to Smolensk. Now, go to sleep, you won't have to be on the watch this time," he said with a suggestion of a smile.

Weary as I was I still remembered a few more things to say to "Larkin" who was by this time somewhat subdued. It was not until I had threatened to report him to the Moscow Government, and had again told him that it was a brutal thing to take advantage of men who were doing their duty under the most difficult circumstances conceivable, that my mind was lightened sufficiently so that I could go to sleep.

Of one thing I had been convinced—the general efficiency of organization which I had encountered again and again in Soviet Russia. The people were universally kind, but with strangers they took no chances. Well, I concluded, they could not have been blamed if they had kept us in jail for a long while, until they had checked up my entire record in Russia, at least. And I was grateful that my prison record amounted to two hours only, thanks to the expedition with which they administer trial to suspects in Red Russia.

Shut up in our coach we sped on to Smolensk the next day. Another twenty-four hours in Smolensk, where I was given permission to proceed to Moscow and again I boarded a train. I had been relayed from one army post to another; from the company to the regiment, from the regiment to the brigade, from the brigade to the division, from the division to the army command, and from the army command to the high command. And after eight days I was almost within reach of Moscow. On the morrow I would be off for Moscow itself.

LENIN AT HIS DESK IN KREMLIN, 1919

CHAPTER IV

MOSCOW

I reached Moscow on Sunday afternoon and was taken at once by "Larkin" to the Foreign Office at the Metropole hotel. As we drove through the picturesque town of many churches we passed great numbers of people enjoying the sunshine. The parks and squares were full of romping children.

In the Foreign Office I was greeted by Litvinoff, who gave me credentials which granted me freedom of action—freedom to go where I pleased and without a guard as long as I remained in Soviet Russia; and Communist life began for me.

The Metropole hotel, like all others in Soviet Russia, had been taken over by the Government. The rooms not occupied by the Foreign Office were used as living rooms by Government employees. The National hotel is used entirely for Soviet workers, and the beautiful residence in which Mirbach, the German ambassador, was assassinated is now the headquarters of the Third International.

No one was allowed to have more than one meal a day. This consisted of cabbage soup, a small piece of fish and black bread, and was served at Soviet restaurants at any time between one o'clock in the afternoon and seven at night. There were a few old cafés still in existence, run by private speculators, where it was possible to purchase a piece of meat at times, but the prices were exorbitant. In the Soviet restaurants ten rubles was charged for the meal, while in the cafés the same kind of meal would have cost from 100 to 150 rubles.

The Soviet restaurants had been established everywhere, in villages and small towns as well as in cities. In the villages and railway stations they were usually in the station building itself or near it. In the cities they were scattered everywhere, so as to be easily accessible to the workers. Some of them were run on the cafeteria plan; in others women carried the food to the tables for the other workers. One entered, showed his credentials to prove that he was a worker and was given a meal check, for which he paid a fixed sum. Needless to say, there was no tipping. I had not the courage to experiment by offering a tip to these dignified, self-respecting women. I think they would have laughed at my "stupid foreign ways" had I done so.

The old café life of Moscow was a thing of the past. If you wished anything to eat at night you had to purchase bread and tea earlier in the day and make tea in your room. This was very simple because the kitchens in hotels were used exclusively for heating water. At breakfast time and all through the evening a stream of people went to the kitchen with pails and pitchers for hot water which they carried to their rooms themselves where they made their tea and munched black bread. There were no maids or bell boys to do these errands for you, and the only service you got in a hotel was that of a maid who cleaned your room each morning.

The working people would buy a pound or two of black bread in the evening on their way home. They had their samovars on which they made tea, and if they felt so inclined ate in the evening. For breakfast they again had tea and black bread like every one else. As a result of this diet hundreds of thousands of people were suffering from malnutrition. The bulk of the people in the city were hungry all the time.

I found the tramway service,—reduced fifty percent because of the lack of fuel,—miserably inadequate for the needs of the population which had greatly increased since Moscow became the capital. The citizens in their necessity have developed the most extraordinary propensities in step-clinging. They swarm on the platforms and stand on one another's feet with the greatest good nature, and then, when there isn't room to wedge in another boot, the late-comers cling to the bodies of those who have been lucky enough to get a foothold, and still others cling to these, until the overhanging mass reaches half-way to the curb. I tried it once myself—and walked thereafter. There were not many automobiles to be seen. The Government had requisitioned all cars. The motors were run by coal oil and alcohol, and the Government had very little of these.

During my second day in Moscow I met some English prisoners walking quite freely in the streets. I went up to a group of three and told them I was an American, and asked how they were getting on. They said they wanted to go home because the food was scarce, but aside from the lack of food they had nothing to complain of.

"Of course food is scarce," said one, "but we get just as much as anyone else. Nobody gets much. You see us walking about the streets. No one is following us. We are free to go where we please. They send us to the theatre three nights a week. We go to the opera and the ballet. That's what they do with all prisoners."

Another broke in enthusiastically to say that if there were only food enough he would be glad to stay in Russia. Several of their pals, they told me, were working in Soviet offices.

They belonged to a detachment of ninety English who had been captured six months before, on the Archangel front. Before they went into action, they said, their commanding officer told each one to carry a hand grenade in his pocket, and if taken prisoner to blow off his head.

"The Bolsheviki," he told us, "would torture us—first they would cut off a finger, then an ear, then the tip of the nose, and they would keep stripping us and torturing us until we died twenty-one days later.

"Well, before we knew it the Bolsheviki had us surrounded. There was nothing to do but surrender—and none of us used his bomb. The Bolsheviks marched us back about ten miles to a barrack, where we were told to sit down. Pretty soon they brought in a samovar and gave us tea and bread, and when we were about half through eating they brought in bundles of pamphlets. The pamphlets were all printed in English, mind you, and they told us why we had been sent to Russia."

I recognized in his description the thing I had seen myself on the Western Front a few days before. I asked him if that was the usual way of treating prisoners.

"Yes," he said, "that's the way they do it. They don't kill you. They just feed you with tea and bread, and this—what they call on the outside 'propaganda' and they say to you, 'you read this stuff for a week,' and you do, and you believe it—you can't help it."

It was bitterly cold in Moscow, though the Bolshevists made light of the September weather and laughed at my complaints. "Stay the winter with us," they said, "and you will learn what cold is." The city was practically without heat. The chill and damp entered my bones and pursued me through the streets and into my bed at night. One can stand prolonged exposure and cold if there is only the sustaining thought of a glowing fire somewhere, and a warm bed. But in Moscow there was no respite from the relentless chill. One was cold all day and all night. The aching pinch of it tore at the nerves. I marvelled at the endurance of the undernourished clerks and officials in the great damp Government office buildings, where it was often colder than in the dry sunshine outside.

All the large department stores and the clothing and shoe shops had been taken over by the Government. Here and there, however, were small private shops, selling goods without regard to Government prices.

The Soviet stores were arranged much like our large department stores. One could go in and buy various commodities, shoes in one department, clothing in another, and so on. Soviet employees had the right at all times to purchase in these stores at Soviet prices. They carried credentials showing they were giving useful service to the Government. Without credentials one could buy nothing—not even food—except from the privately-owned shops.

To these the peasant speculators would bring home-made bread in sacks and sell it to the shop speculators, who in turn demanded as much as eighty rubles a pound. This was the only way of getting bread without credentials because the Government had taken control of the bakeries. In a Soviet store a pound of bread could be bought for ten rubles.

All unnecessary labor in Soviet stores had been eliminated. Young girls and women acted as clerks; very few men were employed in any capacity. The manager, who usually was to be found on the first floor, was a man, and he directed customers to the departments which sold the things they wished to purchase. The elevators were running not only in the stores, but in the office buildings.

White collars and white shirts could be bought in some stores, but they were rationed so that it would have been impossible to buy three or four shirts at one time. The windows in the stores were filled with articles, but there was no attempt to display goods, and there was no advertising.

A shine, a shave and a hair-cut were obtainable at the Soviet barber shops. They were not rationed; one could buy as many of these as desired.

Theatres and operas were open and largely attended in Moscow, and the actors and actresses, as well as the singers, did not seem to mind the cold.

The streets were but dimly lighted, because of the fuel shortage, but I saw and heard of no crimes being committed. I wandered about the city through many of its darkest streets, at all hours of the night, and was never molested. Now and then a policeman demanded my permit, which, when I had shown it, was accepted without question. The city was well policed, the streets fairly clean, and the government was doing everything possible to prevent disease. Orders were issued that all water must be boiled, but as all Russians drink tea this order was not unusual or difficult to carry out.

The telephone and telegraph systems seemed to me unusually good. Connections by telephone between Moscow and Petrograd were obtained in two minutes. Local service was prompt and efficient, and connections with wrong numbers were of rare occurrence.

Many newspapers were being published, the size of all being limited on account of the shortage of paper. In addition to the Government newspapers and the Bolshevist party papers there were papers of opposing parties, notably publications controlled by the Menshevists and the Social Revolutionists.

All of them were free from the advertising of business firms, since the Government had nationalized all trade. Of course there was no "funny page" or "Women's Section."

As soon as news came from the front great bulletins were distributed through the city and posted on the walls of buildings where every one could read them. These bulletins contained the news of both defeat and victory. If prisoners had been taken or a retreat had been necessary, the populace was informed of it frankly. There was no attempt to keep up the "morale" of the civilian population by assuring it that all went well and that victory was certain. Any one in Soviet Russia who accepted the responsibilities of the new order did so knowing that it meant hardship and defeat—for a time.

In Moscow many statues have been erected since the revolution. Skobileff Square,—now called Soviet Square,—has a statue of Liberty which takes the place of the old statue of Skobileff. I saw sculptors at work all over the city, putting in medallions and bas-reliefs, on public buildings. In Red Square, along the Kremlin wall, are the graves of many who fell in the revolution. Sverdlov, formerly president of the executive committee, and a close friend of Lenin, is buried here. I was told that his death had been a great loss to the Soviet Government.

Moscow, like all the other Russian cities I saw, had schools everywhere, art schools, musical conservatories, technical schools, in addition to the regular schools for children.

On "Speculator's Street" in Moscow all kinds of private trading went on without interference. I found this street thronged with shoppers and with members of the old bourgeoisie selling their belongings along the curb; men and women unmistakably of the former privileged classes offering, dress suits, opera cloaks, evening gowns, shoes, hats, and jewelry to any one who would pay them the rubles that they, in turn, must give to the exorbitant speculators for the very necessities of life.

These irreconcilables of the old regime, unwilling to cooperate with the new government and refusing to engage in useful work which would entitle them to purchase their supplies at the Soviet shops, at Soviet prices, were compelled to resort to the speculators and under pressure of the constantly decreasing ruble and the wildly soaring prices, were driven to sacrifice their valuables in order to avoid starvation. Any one who desired and who had the money could buy from the speculators; but one pays dearly for pride in Soviet Russia. The speculators charged seventy-five rubles a pound for black bread that could be bought in the Government shops for ten rubles. The right to buy at the Soviet shops and to eat in the Soviet restaurants was to be had by the mere demonstration of a sincere desire to do useful work of hand or brain. Nevertheless these defenders of the old order still held out—fewer of them every day, to be sure—and the speculators throve accordingly.

It seemed at first glance a strange anomaly. I could see through the windows of the speculator's shops canned goods and luxuries, and even necessities, for which the majority of the population were suffering. I asked why the Government did not put its principles into practice by requisitioning all these stocks and ending the speculation. There were many things in their program, the Bolshevists said, which could not be carried out at once because the energy of the Government was consumed in the mobilization of all available resources for national defence. There were thousands of speculators all over Russia, and it would take a small army to eliminate them entirely. Half measures would only drive them underground where they would be a constant source of irritation and anti-Government propaganda. It was better to let them operate in the open, they said, where they could be kept under observation and restrained within certain limits.

Meanwhile the speculators were eliminating themselves and dragging with them the recalcitrant bourgeoisie on whom they preyed. Hoarded wealth and old finery do not last forever. As the ruble falls and the speculator's prices rise their victims are compelled to sacrifice more and more of their dwindling resources. The Government prices are a standing temptation to reconciliation. Only the obdurate bourgeoisie and the speculators suffer from the depreciation of the ruble. Every two months wages are adjusted to meet depreciation, by a Government commission which acts in conjunction with the Central Federation of All Russian Professional Alliances, representing skilled and unskilled labor. This serves to stabilize the purchasing power of the workers earnings, although in the past unavoidable and absolute dearth of necessities has tended to work against this stabilization.

In the meantime the falling ruble and the avaricious speculator between them drive thousands of the stubborn into the category of useful laborers. Every day brings numbers who have, either through a change of heart, or by economic necessity, been driven to ask for work which will entitle them to their bread and food cards. Thus the Communists, too busy with the military defence of their country to attend to the last measures of expropriation, make use of the irresistible economic forces of the old order and allow the capitalists to expropriate themselves.

LENIN IN SWITZERLAND, MARCH, 1916

I found no Red terror. There was serious restriction of personal liberty and stern enforcement of law and order, as might be expected in a nation threatened with foreign invasion, civil war, counter revolution, and an actual blockade. While I was in Moscow sixty men and seven women were shot for complicity in a counter revolutionary plot. They had arms stored in secret places and had been found guilty of circularizing the soldiers on the Denikin front, telling them that Petrograd and Moscow had both fallen. They made no concealment of their purpose to overthrow the Government and went bravely to their execution. Several days later two bombs were exploded under a building in which a meeting of the Executive Committee of the Communist party was being held. Eleven of the Communists were killed and more than twenty wounded. The cadet counter revolutionists, it was charged, committed this outrage as reprisal for the execution of their comrades. But no terror or persecution followed. Instead great mass meetings were held everywhere to protest against all terrorist acts. Intrigue and propaganda were met with counter propaganda and popular enthusiasm for the Soviet Government.

Before leaving Moscow for Petrograd I applied at the Foreign Office for permission to go to the Kremlin and interview Lenin. I was told that permission would be granted, and an appointment was made for me to meet Lenin at his office at three o'clock on the following day.

CHAPTER V

INTERVIEW WITH LENIN

A quarter of an hour ahead of the hour set for my appointment with Lenin, I hastened to the Kremlin enclosure, the well-guarded seat of the executive government. Two Russian soldiers inspected my pass and led me across a bridge to obtain another pass from a civilian to enter the Kremlin itself and to return to the outside. I had heard that Lenin was guarded by Chinese soldiers, but I looked in vain for a Chinese among the guards that surrounded the Kremlin. In fact I saw but two Chinese soldiers during my entire stay in Soviet Russia.

I mounted the hill and went toward the building where Lenin lives and has his office. At the outer door two more soldiers met me, inspected my passes, and directed me up a long staircase, at the top of which stood two more soldiers. They directed me down a long corridor to another soldier who sat before a door. This one inspected my passes and finally admitted me to a large room in which many clerks, both men and women, were busy over desks and typewriters. In the next room I found Lenin's secretary who informed me that "Comrade Lenin will be at liberty in a few minutes." It was then five minutes before three. A clerk gave me a copy of the *London Times*, dated September 2, 1919, and told me to sit down. While I read an editorial the secretary addressed me and asked me to go into the next room. As I turned to the door it opened, and Lenin stood waiting with a smile on his face.

It was twelve minutes past three, and Lenin's first words were, "I am glad to meet you, and I apologize for keeping you waiting."

Lenin is a man of middle height, close to fifty years of age. He is well proportioned, and very active, physically, in spite of the fact that he carries in his body two bullets fired at him in August, 1918. His head is large, massive in outline, and is set close to his shoulders. His forehead is broad and high, his mouth large, the eyes wide apart and there appears in them at times a very infectious twinkle. His hair, pointed beard, and mustache, have a brown tinge. His face has wrinkles,—said by some to be wrinkles of humor,—but I am inclined to believe them the result of deep study, and of the suffering he endured through long years of exile and persecution. I would not minimize the contribution that his sense of humor has made to these lines and wrinkles, for no man who lacked a sense of humor could have overcome the obstacles he has met.

During our conversation his eyes never left mine. This direct regard was not that of a man who wished to be on guard; it bespoke a frank interest, which seemed to me to say, "We shall be able to tell many things of interest to each other. I believe you to be a friend. In any event we shall have an interesting talk."

He moved his chair close to his desk and turned so that his knees were close to mine. Almost at once he began asking me about the labor movement in America, and from that he went on to discuss the labor situation in other countries. He was thoroughly informed even as to the most recent developments everywhere. I soon found myself asking him questions.

I told him that the press of various countries had been saying that Soviet Russia was a dictatorship of a small minority. He replied, "Let those who believe that silly tale come here and mingle with the rank and file and learn the truth.

"The vast majority of industrial workers and at least one-half of the articulate peasantry are for Soviet rule, and are prepared to defend it with their lives.

"You say you have been along the Western Front," he continued. "You admit that you have been allowed to mingle with the soldiers of Soviet Russia, that you have been unhampered in making your investigation. You have had a very good opportunity to understand the temper of the rank and file. You have seen thousands of men living from day to day on black bread and tea. You have probably seen more suffering in Soviet Russia than you had ever thought possible, and all this because of the unjust war being made upon us, including the economic blockade, in all of which your own country is playing a large part. Now I ask you what is your opinion about this being a dictatorship of the minority?"

I could only answer that from what I had seen and experienced I could not believe that these people, who had found their strength and overthrown a despotic Czar, would ever submit to such privations and sufferings except in defence of a government in which, however imperfect, they had ultimate faith, and which they were prepared to defend against all odds.

"What have you to say at this time about peace and foreign concessions?" I asked.

He answered, "I am often asked whether those American opponents of the war against Russia—as in the first place bourgeois—are right who expect from us, after peace is concluded, not only resumption of trade relations but also the possibility of securing concessions in Russia. I repeat once more that they are right. A durable peace would be such a relief to the toiling masses of Russia that these masses would undoubtedly agree to certain concessions being granted. The granting of concessions under reasonable terms is also desirable to us, as one of the means of attracting into Russia the technical help of the countries which are more advanced in this respect, during the co-existence side by side of Socialist and capitalist states."

In reply to my next question about Soviet power he replied:

"As for the Soviet power, it has become familiar to the minds and hearts of the laboring masses of the whole world which clearly grasped its meaning. Everywhere the laboring masses, in spite of the influence of the old leaders with their chauvinism and opportunism which permeates them through and through, became aware of the rottenness of the bourgeois parliaments and of the necessity of the Soviet power, the power of the toiling masses, the dictatorship of the proletariat, for the sake of the emancipation of humanity from the yoke of capital. And the Soviet power will win in the whole world, however furiously, however frantically the bourgeoisie of all countries may rage and storm.

"The bourgeoisie inundates Russia with blood, waging war upon us and inciting against us the counter revolutionaries, those who wish the yoke of capital to be restored. The bourgeoisie inflict upon the working masses of Russia unprecedented sufferings, through the blockade, and through their help given to the counter revolutionaries, but we have already defeated Kolchak and we are carrying on the war against Denikin with the firm assurance of our coming victory."

In his replies to my last questions he had covered the ground of the others on my list, and since the fifteen minutes allotted to me had extended to more than an hour, I rose to go. I intended to ask him about "nationalization of women." I had never believed the story, and had already discovered that it was false, but I had thought to ask Lenin how the story arose. When I met him and had talked to him something in his face silenced the question. Perhaps it was the mocking humor that seemed ready to flash out of the wrinkled countenance in scathing ridicule, or perhaps it was the sign of long-suffering and profound thought that lay deeper. Whatever it was I did not ask that question. I had seen for myself that women in Soviet Russia are shown a respect and deference far exceeding the superficial politeness which in other countries too often serves to conceal political, economic, and domestic oppression. Women are on an equal footing in all respects with men in Russia, and they enjoy a greater measure of freedom and security than the women of other countries.

He shook hands cordially, and I went away cudgelling my brains to find another figure among the statesmen of the world with whom I might compare him. I could think only of our own Lincoln, whose image came to me, suggested perhaps by the simplicity and plainness of Lenin's attire. Workman's shoes, worn trousers, a soft shirt with a black four-in-hand tie, a cheap office coat, and the kindly strong face and figure,—these were my impressions of the man.

He works from fifteen to eighteen hours a day, receiving reports, keeping in touch with the situation all over Russia, attending committee meetings, making speeches, always ready to give anyone advice, counsel, or suggestion. He lives with his wife who is most loyal and devoted, in the same building where he has his office, in two modestly furnished rooms.

Soviet rule has captured not only the imagination, but also the intellects of the majority of the rank and file of Russia. Lenin is looked upon as the highest representative of that principle; he is trusted and he is loved. I was told that so many people come to see him from the outlying districts, men, women, and children, that it is impossible for him to see them all. They bring him bread, eggs, butter, and fruit,—and he turns all into the common fund.

Sometime in the future, whatever may happen to Soviet Russia, the true life of Lenin will be written, and when it is he will stand out as one of history's most remarkable men.

EXTERIOR AND INTERIOR OF LENIN'S HOME IN ZURICH

CHAPTER VI

"WHO IS LENIN?"

Many conflicting stories were told and published about Lenin after the Bolshevist uprising in November, 1917. I decided to ascertain for myself during the two weeks I spent in Switzerland before going into Russia what the people of that country knew about him.

Lenin arrived in Switzerland in September, 1914, and left for Russia in March, 1917, with thirty other Russians, on the much-talked-of train that went through Germany with the sanction of the Kaiser.

A whole myth has grown up around Lenin since his return to Russia. He was a German agent; he was sent from Switzerland to Russia through Germany; he went for the express purpose of fomenting revolution in order to break down the morale of the Russian Army and to make it possible for German militarism to conquer. Document after document was printed to prove that this man was mercenary, that he was cold-blooded, without ideals of any kind, and that he had received millions in money from the Germans, whose plans he conscientiously carried out,—at least in connection with the disorganization of the Russian Army. While in Switzerland for two years during the war, he lived in luxury, always had plenty of money which was supplied from an unknown source, later discovered to be the banks of Germany.

I found when I went to Zurich that Lenin had passed the greater part of his time when in Switzerland in that town, and had lived in the poor quarter of the city. The house in which he and his wife lived, No. 14 Spiegelgasse, is on a very narrow street running down to the quay. They lived in one room on the second floor of this house. Their meagre furniture included a table, a washstand, two plain chairs, a small stove, a bed, a couch, and a petrol lamp. The room had a plaster ceiling and was unpapered, the bare board walls seeming most bleak. A cheap, dingy carpet covered the floor. The room was accessible only through a dark narrow corridor. On the same floor were three other rooms, two of which were occupied by two families, and the third was used as a common kitchen by every one. In this kitchen Lenin's wife, who was his constant companion, only secretary and assistant, prepared their frugal meals and carried them to their room.

For these quarters Lenin paid thirty-eight francs a month, the equivalent of six dollars and sixty cents in American money.

I was told by many people who had known him in Zurich that Lenin seemed to wish to mingle only with working people there. His revolutionary friends took great pride in saying, "He never spent any time with mere intellectual reformers." They told me that much of his time was passed in the Swiss Workers' Assembly, where he talked to every one, but never made any speeches. He did speak, however, on many occasions in the Russian Assembly in Zurich.

His income was derived from articles written for Russian party papers. Before leaving for Russia he closed his account at a Zurich bank and drew out the balance on deposit there, which amounted to twenty-five francs.

For a short time while in Switzerland Lenin lived in Berne, in two rooms. I met the woman at whose Pension he dined while there. She said she had served Lenin, his wife, and his wife's mother midday dinners while they stayed there. The price of those meals was eighty centimes each,—approximately sixteen cents. She informed me that they prepared their own breakfasts and evening meals.

The proprietor of the Wiener café, a coffee house located on the corner of Schrittfaren and Gurtengasse in Berne, told me that he remembered Lenin well, that he had come into his place on a number of occasions for a cup of coffee. "He spent most of his time here reading the papers and talking with the waiters," he said, and described him as always being poorly dressed.

None of these simple people thought of Lenin as a person of any greater importance than themselves. He was one of them, a serious student who mingled with working people, eager to tell them of their importance in the political world.

When the Czar was overthrown and the Kerensky Government came into power, a committee of all the Socialist parties in Switzerland except the "Social Patriots" made an effort to assist in getting Russian exiles back to their own country. This committee collected the money for the transportation of the exiles. They endeavored to secure from France, England, and Switzerland permission for their passage through Archangel to Petrograd, but the Allied governments denied this permit. Then the Swiss Socialists entered into negotiations with the German Government to secure passage through Germany. On condition that an equal number of civilian prisoners then held in Russia be allowed to return to Germany, the German Government agreed to the passage of the immigrants through Germany.

The following statement, signed by the members of the Committee, is given in full, even to the peculiar English of the translation.

"The Return of the Russian Emigrants."

In view of the fact that the Entente newspapers have recently published a series of sensational and false accounts and articles regarding the return of the Russian comrades (Lenin, Zinovieff and others) branding them as accomplices and agents of Imperial Germany, as coworkers of the German Government. Simultaneously the German and Austrian press is attempting to represent these Russian revolution comrades as pacifists and separate peace advocates, we therefore deem it necessary to publish the following explanation under the Signature of the Comrades of France, Germany, Poland and Switzerland to whitewash the Comrades that departed to Russia.

We the undersigned are aware of the hindrances which the governments of

the Entente are putting in the way of our Russian Internationalists in their departure. They learned of the conditions which the German Government has placed
before them for their passage through to Sweden.

Not having the slightest doubt as to the fact, that the German Government is
speculating by it to strengthen the one-sided anti-war tendencies in Russia, we
declare:

The Russian Internationalists who during the whole war period have been
combating in the sharpest possible manner imperialism in general and the German imperialism in particular, and who are now going to Russia in order to work
there for the cause of the Revolution, will thus be aiding the proletarians of all
countries as well, and particularly the German and Austrian working class by encouraging them to the revolutionary struggle against their own governments.

Nothing can be more stimulating and inspiring in this respect than the exam-
ple of the heroic struggle on the part of the Russian proletariat. For that reason
we the undersigned Internationalists of France, Switzerland, Poland and Germany
consider it to be not only the right but a duty on the part of our Russian comrades
to use the opportunity for the voyage to Russia, which is offered to them.

We wish them the best results in the struggle against the Imperialistic policy
of Russian bourgeoisie, which constitutes a part of our general struggle for the
liberation of the working class, for the social revolution.

Bern, April 7, 1917.

> Paul Hantstein, Germany
> Henri Guilbeaux, France
> F. Loriot, France
> Bronski, Poland
> F. Platten, Swiss

The above declaration has received the full approval and signature of the following Scandinavian comrades:

> Lindhagen, Mayor of Stockholm
> Strom, Congressman and Secretary of S. D. P. of Sweden
> Karleson, Congressman and President of Trades Union Council
> Fure Nerman, Editor *Politiken*
> Tchilbun, Editor *Steukleken*
> Hausen, Norway.

The next train left in May, 1917, carrying three hundred Russians, and another three hundred went through Germany in July, 1917. In July the French and
English governments finally granted permission for a train-load to pass through
those countries to Archangel and thence to Russia. This trip lasted two months. I
learned that the May and July trains also carried to Russia many active Menshevists, supporters of the Kerensky Government.

In August another group tried to return, but because Kerensky protested, the
French and English notified this group that they must have passports from Russia.
It was then impossible to go through Germany because of battles going on along

the front. They did not get to Russia until December, after the Russian-German armistice.

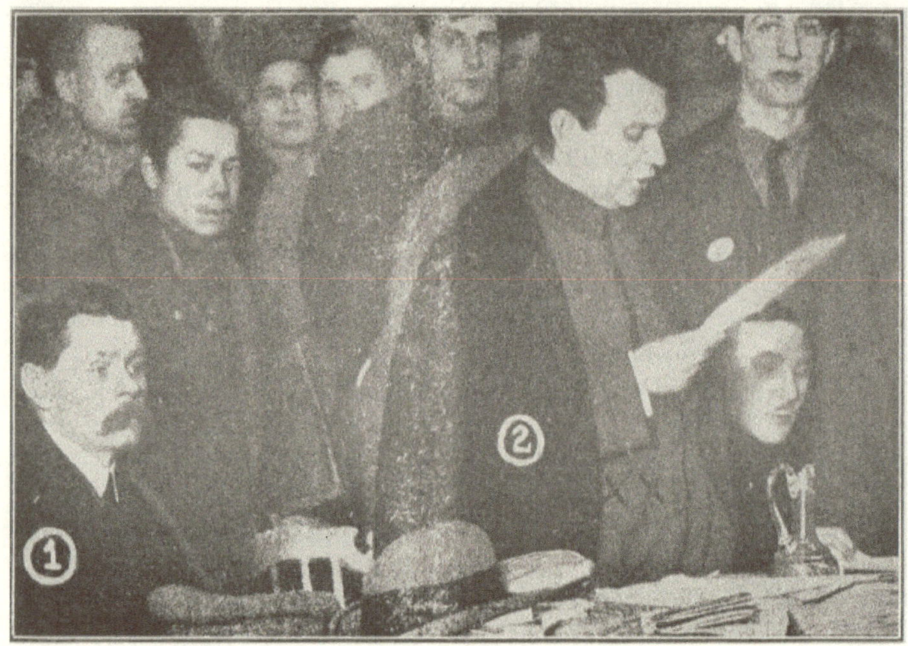

1. GORKY. 2. ZINOVIEFF

Zinovieff, in an address to the Petrograd Soviet, September 6, 1918, told the story of the fabled armored train as follows:

"In March, 1917, Lenin returned to Russia. Do you remember the cries that went up about the 'armored train' on which Lenin and the rest of us returned? In reality Lenin felt a profound hatred of German imperialism. He hated it no less than he hated any other brand of imperialism.... When a prominent member of the Scheidemann party attempted to enter our car (which was not armored) in order to 'greet' us, he was told, at Lenin's suggestion, that we would not speak to traitors and that he would be sparing himself insult if he refrained from trying to enter. The Mensheviki and the Social Revolutionists, who were rather stubborn at first, later on came back to Russia in the same way (more than three hundred of them). Lenin put the matter simply, 'All bourgeois governments are brigands: we have no choice since we cannot get into Russia by any other way.'"

I found the following in a long article of appreciation written by Ernest Nobs, editor of the Swiss *Volkrecht*, published in Zurich in December, 1917.

"One who has seen the last winter, the medium-sized, square-built man, with a somewhat yellowish face and sharp, sparkling and flashing Mongol eyes, as he was steering towards some library in a wornout ulster coat, with a heap of books under his arm, could hardly foresee in him the future Russian premier."

In the address mentioned on the foregoing page, delivered at the time Lenin was shot, Zinovieff said:

Vladimir Ilyich Ulyanoff (Lenin) was born on April 10, 1870, in the city of Simbirsk. His father, who was of peasant descent, was employed as Director of Public Schools in the Volga region. His elder brother, Alexander Ulyanoff was executed by Czar Alexander III. From that time on his mother showered all her tender affections on Vladimir Ilyich, and Lenin in his turn dearly loved her. Living as an emigrant, an exile, persecuted by the Czar's Government, Lenin used to tear himself away from the most urgent tasks to go to Switzerland to see his mother in her last days. She died in 1913.

Upon his graduation from high school (gymnasium) Vladimir Ilyich entered the law school at the Kazan University. The universities of the capitals were closed to him because he was the brother of an executed revolutionist. A month after his entry he was expelled from the University for participation in a revolutionary movement of the students. It was not until four years had gone by that he was allowed to resume his studies. The legal career held no attractions for Lenin. His natural inclinations lay towards the field of revolutionary activity.... When he was expelled from the Kazan University he went to Petrograd. The first phase of his activities was confined to student circles. A year or two later he created in Petrograd the first 'workmen's circles' and a little later crossed swords on the literary arena with the old leader of the Populists, N. K. Mikhailovsky. Under the *nom de plume* of Ilyin, Lenin published a series of brilliant articles on economics which at once won him a name.

In Petrograd he, with other workers, founded the 'Union for the Emancipation of the Working Class,' and conducted the first labor strikes, writing meanwhile leaflets and pamphlets remarkable for their simplicity of style and clarity. These were printed on a hectograph and distributed.... Very often now workers coming from far off Siberia or the Ural to the All-Russian Congress of Soviets recall to him their activities together in the early 90's. They recognize that he was their teacher, the first to kindle the spark of communism in them.

In the 90's Lenin was sentenced to a long prison term and then exiled. While in exile he devoted himself to scientific and literary activities, and wrote a number of books. One of these reached a circle of exiles in Switzerland, among whom were Plekhanoff, Axelrod, and Zasulich, who welcomed Lenin as the harbinger of a coming season, and who could not find words of praise sufficiently strong. Another book, a truly scientific one, won the praise of Professor Maxim Kovalevsky of the Paris School of Social Science. "What a good professor Lenin would have made!" he said.

Vladimir Ilyich languished in exile like a caged lion. The only thing that saved him was the fact that he was leading the life of a scientist. He used to spend fifteen hours daily in the library over books, and it is not without reason that he is now one of the most cultured men of our time.... In 1901 Lenin, together with a group of intimate friends, began the publication of a newspaper, *Iskra, The Spark*. This paper not only waged a political struggle, but it carried on vast organizing activities, and Lenin was the soul of the organizing committee.

Lenin's wife, Nadezhda Konstantinovna Krupskaya Ulyanova was the secretary of *Iskra* and the secretary of the organizing committee. Throughout Lenin's activities as an organizer a considerable share of the credit is due to his wife. All the correspondence was in her charge. At one time she was in communication with entire Russia. Who did not know her? Martov in his bitter controversy with Lenin once called her "Secretary of Lenin, the Super-Center."...

In the summer of 1905 the first conference of the Bolsheviki was called. Officially it was known as the Third Conference of the Revolutionary Social Democratic Labor Party. This conference laid the corner-stone for the present Communist Party.... In the revolution of 1905 Lenin's part was enormous, although he was residing in Petrograd illegally and was forbidden by the party to attend its meetings openly.

Vladimir Ilyich was exiled for the second time in 1907. In Geneva, and later in Paris, chiefly through the efforts of Lenin, the newspapers, *The Proletarian* and *The Social Democrat* were founded. Complete decadence was reigning all around. Obscene literature took the place of art literature. The spirit of nihilism permeated the sphere of politics. Stolypin was indulging in his orgies. And it seemed as if there was no end to all this.

At such times true leaders reveal themselves. Vladimir Ilyich suffered at that time, as he did right along in exile, the greatest personal privations. He lived like a pauper, he was sick and starved, especially when he lived in Paris. But he retained his courage as no one else did. He stood firmly and bravely at his post. He alone knew how to weld together a circle of gallant fighters to whom he used to say, "Do not lose your courage. The dark days will pass, a few years will elapse, and the proletarian revolution will be revived."

For two years Lenin scarcely left the national library at Paris, and during this time he accomplished such a large amount of work that even those very professors who were attempting to ridicule his philosophic works admitted that they could not understand how a man could do so much.

The years 1910–11 brought a fresh breeze to stir the atmosphere. It became clear in 1911 that the workers' movement was beginning to revive. We had in Petrograd a paper, the *Star*, (*Zviezda*), and in Moscow a magazine, *Thought* (*Mysl*), and there was a small labor representation in the Duma. And the principal worker both on these papers and for the Duma representation was Lenin. He taught the principles of revolutionary parliamentarism to the labor deputies in the Duma. "You just get up and tell the whole of Russia plainly about the life of the worker. Depict the horrors of the capitalist galleys, call upon the workers to revolt, fling into the face of the black Duma the name of 'scoundrels and exploiters.'" At first they found this strange advice. The entire Duma atmosphere was depressing, its members and ministers met in the Tauride palace, clad in full dress suits. They learned their lessons however.

In 1912 we started to lead a new life. At the January conference of that year the Bolsheviki reunited their ranks which had been broken up by the counter revolution. At the request of the new Central Executive Committee Lenin and myself went to Krakov (Cracow, in Galicia). There comrades began to come to us from Petrograd, Moscow, and elsewhere. I recall the first large general meeting of the Petrograd metal workers, in 1913. Two hours after our candidates had been elected to the executive committee Lenin received a wire from the metal workers, congratulating him upon the victory. He lived a thousand versts away from Petrograd, yet he was the very soul of the workers of Petrograd. It was a repetition of what took place in 1906–7 when Lenin lived in Finland, and we used to visit him every week to receive counsel from him. From the little village of Kuokalla, in Finland, he steered the labor movement of Petrograd.

In 1915–17 Lenin was leading a very peculiar life in Switzerland. The war and the collapse of the International had a very marked effect on him. Many of his comrades who knew him well were surprised at the changes wrought in him by the war.

He never felt very tenderly toward the bourgeoisie, but with the beginning of the war he began to nurture a concentrated, keen, intense hatred for them. It seemed that his very countenance had changed.

In Zurich he resided in the poorest quarter, in the flat of a shoemaker. He appeared to be after every single proletarian, trying as it were to get hold of him and explain that the war was an imperialistic slaughter.... Lenin has always understood what enormous difficulties would arise before the working class after it had seized all power. From the first days of his arrival in Petrograd he carefully observed the economic disruption. He valued his acquaintance with every bank employee, striving to penetrate into all the details of the banking business. He was well aware of the provisioning problem, and of other difficulties. In one of his most remarkable books he dwells at length on these difficulties. On the question of the nationalization of banks, in the domain of the provisioning policy and on the war question Lenin has said the decisive word. He worked out concretely the plan of practical measures to be adopted in all domains of national life, long before October 25, (November 7), 1917. The plan is clear, concrete, distinct, like all his works....

ZINOVIEFF PRESIDENT OF THE PETROGRAD SOVIET

CHAPTER VII

PETROGRAD

I arrived at the Nicolai station in Petrograd on the 24th of September, from Moscow, and went at once to the Astoria hotel on St. Isaac's Square at the farther end of Nevsky Prospekt. As we drove along the thoroughfare I noticed workmen tearing out the wooden paving-blocks which covered that famous street, and recalled having read in New York papers that whole streets in Petrograd had been torn up and used for fuel. This seemed credible enough, even desirable, I thought, as I recalled the shivering nights I had spent in Russia. When my droshky came nearer to the crew of workers I saw worn and broken blocks piled to one side; in their places new blocks had been put in. Two days later I walked along this same thoroughfare from one end to the other, still looking for unmended gaps in the paving. My search was vain. And the pavements of the side streets, on which I walked miles during my stay in Petrograd, were in good condition.

Many of the shops along Nevsky Prospekt were closed and boarded up, and those that remained open had but few wares on their shelves. The large stores, however, now converted into Soviet stores, were all open and contained a goodly supply of various commodities, but the bright-colored toys that used to fill the shop windows of Petrograd had entirely disappeared. Apparently the peasants of Russia, busy with weightier matters, had found no time to carve grotesque wooden figures and charming dolls and the other gayly-colored toys they know so well how to make. The Russian child who does not have these toys left over from the old days has to do without.

Whatever beautiful things Russia still had, however, were placed in the stores along with the necessities. They were not regarded as luxuries for the few. Art belongs to every one in Soviet Russia.

I learned that the high wall which used to surround the Winter Palace of the Czar had been torn down, and when I asked why this had been done, was told that there was a beautiful garden back of this wall, and since "beauty should not be hidden from the people," they had torn down the wall so that all might see the garden. The palace itself was unoccupied. Its art treasures had been removed to Moscow, and placed in museums there. It was planned to make a museum of the palace later.

On my second day in Petrograd I went out to Smolny Institute, a large stone structure overlooking the Neva, formerly a school for the daughters of the aristocracy, now the office building of the officials and workers of the Northern Commune and Petrograd Soviet.

In front of the institute there was set up a large statue of Karl Marx. It looked impressive enough from a distance. But when I passed on my way into the building and looked back at the statue I discovered Karl Marx—a silk hat in his hand. I have not yet been able to get over my memory of the great economist standing there, heroically erect, before the headquarters of the workingmen's government, holding a silk hat.

In Smolny Institute I met Zinovieff, president of the Petrograd Soviet, a curly-haired, impetuous Jew, full of energy and with a deep understanding of the Russian revolutionary movement. He has been a life-long friend of Lenin and was his companion in exile. I found him distrustful at first, but very cordial when convinced that my intentions were honest.

"Do you still talk about nationalization of women in America?" he asked me with a broad grin. He was the only official in Soviet Russia who ever mentioned the subject to me.

Later in the day I attended a meeting of the Petrograd Soviets which included representatives of all unions, army, navy and peasants. They were assembled in the Tauride Palace, where the Duma met formerly. A decree for compulsory education for adults was under consideration, and Zinovieff spoke for the adoption of the decree. I could not, of course, understand his impassioned address, which subsequent translation revealed to be a clear analysis of the whole educational problem. He has a high-pitched voice, which grated on my ears sometimes, but rang with earnestness and conviction. The decree, which is now in effect, was passed by a practically unanimous vote.

It provided that after November 1, 1919, all adults of the Northern Commune unable to read and write would have to attend public school classes two hours daily for six months, at the end of which time those unable to pass the examinations were to be denied the right to work. For their hours of study the decree provided that they be paid wages at the rate in effect in their branches of industry.

For those illiterates in occupations requiring eight hours labor, the working day was reduced to six, giving them the opportunity to spend the full two hours in school. The six-hour day in force in the hazardous occupations was reduced to four hours.

Soviet officials informed me that passage of the decree did not mean that those who were unable to assimilate knowledge would be denied the right to work. That disciplining would be invoked only for those capable ones who wilfully refused to study. The measure was but one of the efforts of the Soviet Government to hasten the development of the intellectual side of the people's life and to raise culture in general. Under Czars there were few public schools, and these were inefficiently conducted. Seventy-five percent of the people could not read or write.

I inquired about the "Red Terror" in Petrograd. "Yes," I was informed, "there were two or three days of Red Terror in August, 1918, when Lenin was shot, in Moscow." The rank and file were devoted to this man, and when they heard of the attempt on his life they turned loose, and it took three days of hard work on the part of the government officials and the government party members to stop the rush of the mob. Probably two thousand were killed, and during the six weeks that Lenin lay between life and death great crowds of working people watched the bulletins from his physicians that were posted on walls in all parts of the city from day to day. I was told that quite aside from his value to the government itself, it was a godsend to Russia that he survived, because his death would have meant an uprising that would have spared no human being believed to be in opposition to Lenin and the Soviet Government. Even Zinovieff is reported to have lost his head for a little time, when he heard of the precarious condition of his old friend and comrade.

A Russian friend of mine in America had asked me to look for his father who lived two or three blocks from St. Isaac's Square when last heard from four years before.

I found the old man in his place of business—a picture frame store. He lived with his wife in two or three rooms in the rear. He had been in business for years, and was one of the bourgeoisie of the olden days. When I asked him if he had been disturbed by the Bolsheviki he said that during the two years since the revolution his store had been visited once by the authorities—an officer came to inquire for the address of some person living in the immediate neighborhood.

I asked him how he liked the new regime. "I don't like it because food is scarce and prices high." He showed me a small picture frame. "Before the war I could sell this for 70 kopecks, now I must charge 40 rubles,—but then maybe it was the war and not the revolution that caused the high prices,—I don't know."

He took me down the street three blocks to visit his daughter, so that when I returned to America I could assure my friend that his sister, too, was safe. She and her husband were both working for the Soviet Government and had but one complaint to make, "scarcity of food." She was a teacher in one of the Soviet schools. They had two beautiful boys; the elder was studying sculpture in a Soviet art school, the younger was still in the grades. I asked this most intelligent and refined woman whether the Bolshevists had broken up the homes in Petrograd. She smiled and said, "Do they believe that in America?" When I had to answer that "some do," she replied, "Please tell them it does not show intelligence to believe such things."

I talked to three or four of the business men along the Nevsky Prospekt who were still clinging to their little shops, with their pitiful stocks of goods. These people have remained undisturbed for reasons I have already explained. In substance they all said the same thing: "It is terrible,—terrible. Before long we must quit business. The Bolshevists are setting up what they call 'Soviet' stores. The people don't come to us now,—only a few of our old customers. The Soviet stores control the products and undersell us. Russia is doomed. We want to go away. How is it in America?"

The last cry of the private shopkeeper in Russia! Some day when the war is over and Russia is doing business with the rest of the world, these same shopkeepers will probably find the Soviet stores more attractive even than their own. They may remember, with no regret, their constant struggle to survive competition. Doubtless they will get behind the counters of the Soviet stores, as many of their kind have already done, and there find security of employment and compensation, and in the knowledge that they are rendering a real service to the New Russia they will find an adequate substitute for the stimulation of "private enterprise."

CHICHERIN COMMISSAR OF FOREIGN AFFAIRS

With the removal of the capital to Moscow, the sending of thousands of workers to the army, the voluntary emigration to the villages of thousands of others, and the exodus of the bourgeoisie to Scandinavia, France, England and even America, Petrograd has probably one half the population it had under the Czar.

Moscow had gained, however, during the same period in greater proportion than Petrograd lost.

Tram cars were running more regularly than in Moscow, so far as I could observe. The streets were poorly lighted, as in Moscow, and for the same reason. All automobiles had been requisitioned by the army and were used mostly for trucking. The city was policed by women in daytime, by men at night. It was rather startling to encounter a woman policeman with a rifle on her shoulder, but the people took it for granted, and I was told that the women were quite as efficient as the men. In spite of poor lighting, Petrograd is as safe as Moscow at night—or as safe as New York or Chicago, for that matter. Prostitution has lost its clientele. Thousands of women from the streets have found decent employment in various institutions of the Soviet Government, and are able to lead independent, normal lives.

I visited one of the large textile industries, which was in full operation, employing probably three thousand men and women. They were making civilian suits and overcoats and winter coats for the soldiers. Motor lorries drove up and carried away thousands of these winter coats for shipment to the soldiers at the front.

Some of the factories were closing down through lack of fuel. I asked what would become of the workers who were thrown out of employment, and was told that pending their re-employment they would be given "out of work" cards showing that their idleness was not voluntary, and the government would continue to pay them their regular wages.

I visited Maxim Gorky in his modest apartment near the Fortress of Peter and Paul. Gorky is typical of a large class of the intellectuals. Two years ago he was a bitter opponent of Bolshevism, and his writings violently attacked the government.

Of artistic rather than political temperament, and strongly pacifist, he was sickened by the killing on both sides. Since then, however, he has come to the support of the Soviet Government. His tribute to the constructive ability of the Soviet leaders was issued over his signature a year ago, and has been widely circulated.

I had been told that Maxim Gorky was suffering from tuberculosis, and after all the misery I had seen in Soviet Russia because of the lack of food, I expected to find him emaciated. Instead, he was vigorous and healthy. He stood before me tall, powerful, with a slight bend in his shoulders. He seemed with his mass of gray hair like some huge and fearless animal.

There was sadness in his voice and his gray eyes when he spoke of Russia's suffering. Gorky himself was a child of the streets, and he feels keenly the suffering of the people.

But it was when he spoke of the future of his country that he was the true Russian. He told me he believed in the invincible spirit of the Russian masses and their determination to defend "their revolution." He dwelt with pride upon the accomplishments of individual workers, whose native genius had been set free from the old bondage. I was surprised to find the interest he took in the industries. In one factory just outside of Petrograd, he told me, they were extracting sugar from the sawdust of certain woods by a process discovered by a workman. With equal enthusiasm he told me of another worker who had perfected a method of preserving fish nets so that their durability had been increased four hundred percent.

He told me a manifesto would soon be issued to the world, coming from a number of Russian scientists of established reputation, setting forth the scientific achievements accomplished under Soviet rule.

"Under two years of Soviet rule," Gorky said, "there have been more discoveries made in Russia and there has been more progress in general than previously in twenty years under Czarism."

The greatest joy that Gorky finds in his work for the Soviet Government is in the tremendous task of preserving the art of old Russia and creating new art. Even in the throes of the revolution when Gorky opposed the Bolshevik rule, he was working with the government to preserve the old art.

Under his direction a museum was established in a fine structure, wherein were stored thousands of art treasures recovered during the revolution. Bourgeoisie who fled to other countries left their unoccupied homes full of beautiful things. The Soviet Government took possession of these homes at once and removed valuable art to the museum. Manifestos were sent broadcast appealing to the people to preserve these things which were now theirs. In Petrograd the following bulletin, under the title "Appeal for the Preservation of Works of Art," appeared:

"Citizens! The old landlords have gone. Behind them remains a tremendous inheritance. Now it belongs to the whole people. Guard this inheritance; take care of the palaces. They will stand as the palaces of the art of the whole people. Preserve the pictures, the statues, the buildings—these are a concentration of the spiritual force of yourselves and of your forefathers. Art is that beauty which men of talent have been able to create even under the lash of despotism. Do not touch a single stone, safeguard monuments, buildings, ancient things, and documents. All these are your history, your pride."

"But it was impossible to save everything," Gorky told me. "There were the soldiers and the peasants, who had never had a chance to see any of these beautiful things in the past. The people did not wish to destroy these things. They only threw away what seemed worthless to them. One priceless painting was found in a garbage can. But it was found and brought back by the people themselves. And now it is in the museum where every one may see it."

Gorky is head of the "World Literature Publishing House," a vast institution organized by the Soviet Government to publish the best literary and scientific productions of all countries in popular editions for the Russian masses. A great staff of literary and professional men and women are enrolled in this work. Already about six hundred books have been edited and are ready for publication, although only thirty volumes had been printed when the work had to stop on account of the lack of paper. As soon as paper is available they hope to begin printing millions of volumes in editions which will be within the reach of all the Russian people.

In addition to this work Gorky has been devoting much time to the preparation of a series of motion-picture scenarios, composed with scientific historical exactness, showing the history of man from the Stone Age down through the Middle Ages to the time of Louis XVI of France, and finally to the present day. This work was begun in July 1919, and when I talked with Gorky in September of the same year, he told me that they had already finished twenty-five scenarios. He described the extraordinary difficulties under which the work was going forward; the actors and actresses who were often undernourished, persevered over all obstacles, inspired by an enthusiasm which Gorky thought would have been impossible in any other country. The Soviet Government was aiding the production in every way. The best actors and actresses in the country had been enlisted in this work along with historians and scientists. The films were being sent into the remote towns and villages, and thousands of small theatres already were being built.

The motion picture theatres in general in Petrograd were not showing the ordinary romances that we see in this country in films. The motion picture was used largely for educating the people and showing the development of industry, the proper care of children and the advantages of sanitary conditions. Russia is in great need of education so far as sanitation is concerned. In the large cities the sanitation is modern, but in smaller towns and in the villages the people have no idea of a sewage system.

The theatre of Soviet Russia had already been organized throughout the country at the time of my visit. The production of plays and scenarios was included in the educational program of the government. The theatres were organized into one corporation and subsidized by the Soviet Government, which did not, however, interfere in any way with the artistic work of the producers. I saw Schiller's "Robbers" and Gorky's "Lower Depths" produced wonderfully. The people crowded to the theatres. The first four performances each week are set aside for the Soviet workers.

Gorky assured me that the elements opposed to Soviet rule "do not find any support among the rank and file. The working class strongly supports the Soviets, and most of the peasants approve, although the village youth is still indifferent."

The Jewish people were playing an important part in the revolutionary reconstruction of the country, Gorky said, but added that he did not mean the class of Jews who had been influential in the old régime. The Jews who had come forward under the revolution were the ones who had formerly been kept within the pale. They felt that a new freedom had been offered them by the Soviet Government, that they would be treated as brothers, and so they were rendering valuable constructive service.

"If they would only leave us alone," he cried out bitterly. "Tell America for the sake of humanity to leave Russia alone." His words fairly burned as he sat there and talked, emphasizing each phrase with a gesture of his clenched fists. "Tell them to leave us alone. I know quite well that there are many persons in America who have no vision of this Russia, who have no comprehension of what Russia is. But after all, you have a few enlightened people in America. Please tell them that

Russia is not Central Africa, without civilization or statesmanship. Russia is well able to take care of herself."

CHAPTER VIII
BOLSHEVIK LEADERS—BRIEF SKETCHES

TROTZKY

Almost inseparable from the name of Lenin, in the minds of Americans, is that of Trotzky, Minister of War, whose history is well known here. He was Minister of Foreign Affairs up to the time of the signing of the Brest-Litovsk Treaty, when it became necessary to mobilize an army to protect Soviet Russia from foreign invasion, and he was made Minister of War. He took hold of a badly disorganized and worse discouraged army, and through his own hard work, and with the assistance of others, built up an army probably better than any other in the world today.

While in Moscow I heard him address a gathering of some two thousand women, in the Labor Temple—formerly a noblemen's club. He had just returned from the front, and was still wearing his suit of plain khaki and high boots. He reviewed the work of the Red Army, recounting its victories and defeats.

A well-set figure, with black eyes flashing through a pair of thick glasses; a wealth of jet black hair brushed back from a high forehead; dark moustache and small beard; his whole face tanned from being in the open with the troops, he paced the platform from one end to the other, like a caged lion. When he spoke of the counter-revolutionary forces his voice resounded through the hall, filled with scorn, and his face wore a look that was uncanny. The next moment his expression changed, and lowering his voice he spoke in soothing tones of the heroism and devotion of the soldiers of the Red Army.

I could understand at the end of his forty minutes' address what Colonel Raymond Robins meant when he said: "Trotzky is a great orator." He is undoubtedly the most convincing I have ever heard, and I have heard many in several countries. He seems to tug at his listeners until they find themselves leaning forward so as not to miss a single word. The history of this man's life and activities would make an interesting book. I hope it will be written.

CHICHERIN

As Minister of Foreign Affairs, Trotzky was succeeded by Chicherin. He is a tall, slightly stooped figure, about fifty years old, with eyes that burn like coals. He is emaciated from hunger and from hard work. Never a day goes by but Chicherin can be found in his office from twelve to sixteen hours of the time, working with quiet determination and zeal. I saw him in his office at the Metropole two or three times, and was captivated by his kind and gentle manner.

"Yes," he said to me, "we want peace and are ready to conclude at once. Concessions are still here for American capital. Leases can be had for forty-nine years. All we ask is that the Russian labor laws shall prevail here and the Government shall not be interfered with. There is flax here, and timber and many other things that the people of your country want.

"Go back to America and tell them to leave us alone. Just let us get our breath and turn our energies into productive work."

They all said that, Chicherin and many other Commissars. All dwelt upon the need for technical assistance. They look forward to the day when they will be able to apply the best technical and scientific experience of the world to the solution of their problems. They need experts in all lines and of all grades, from simple mechanicians to the most highly trained laboratory specialists.

LITVINOFF ASSISTANT COMMISSAR OF FOREIGN AFFAIRS

LITVINOFF

Litvinoff is a solidly built, jovial, and very astute Lithuanian. He was one of the Collegium in the foreign office under Chicherin, and was the Soviet ambassador in England after the revolution. Later he was sent back to Russia by the British Government. He is an equally shrewd business man and diplomat, and looks more like a British member of parliament than a Russian Bolshevik. He has a keen sense of humor and fun, but takes his duties very seriously. He is the type of man often seen among directors of great enterprises in America, putting through "big deals." One imagines that if he chose to sell his services to a capitalist organization or state he could easily become a "big man."

He was my first host in Moscow, and was very kind and helpful in giving me all the information and assistance possible.

MADAME KOLLONTAY

I met Madame Kollontay in the National Hotel, three or four days after I arrived in Moscow. She is a beautiful, cultured woman, and an excellent speaker. She had just returned from a tour of the southern part of Russia, where she had been establishing schools and organizing homes for the aged, and informed me that the children are so enthusiastic that they do not want to go home when the day's session is over. "There is a feeling of solidarity among them," she said. "They are being educated without the feeling of property of any kind. The psychology of the people has so changed since the revolution that the old order could not last even if it were to be restored," she said "and if the Allies would only withdraw their armies and stop supporting the counter-revolutionary forces Russia could recoup herself without outside aid of any kind."

Asked about the devotion of the people to Lenin she replied that while he was deeply loved and respected the people were not following him blindly, and that their devotion was due to the fact that they realized that he stood always for their best interests.

Madame Kollontay has spent several years in America and asked me about many of her friends in this country. She said she hoped to be able to return at some future time.

MADAME BALABANOVA

Madame Balabanova, secretary of the Third International, which has headquarters at Moscow, is an Italian, not over five feet tall, elderly, but full of fire and spirit. She speaks many languages, including fluent English. I met her on several occasions in Moscow. She reminded me that there was much work to be done, and that the revolution had not ended with the overthrowing of the old order. "We are building the new society," she said, "but it is slow work because of the necessity of converting the country into an armed camp to repel invasion, but when the war stops we will show the world what Soviet rule can do for the oppressed."

She said she hoped to go back to Italy sometime, but presumed it would be impossible, at least until that and other countries had recognized that the Russians and those in sympathy with them were human beings and not "carriers of contagion."

She is a wonderful speaker and an extremely energetic and hard working little woman, much admired and respected by her colleagues.

I once accompanied her on a visit to a hospital, where she spoke to wounded soldiers. More than two hundred convalescent soldiers made up her audience. They lay on their cots or sat in wheel-chairs, some of them armless or with but one arm, others with one leg shot off, and many with ugly head wounds. They greeted Madame Balabanova cheerily, and listened almost eagerly to her story of what was going on at the front and in the country generally. When she had finished her address there was a silence, and then from all the men came the deep singing of the *Internationale*.

BUCHARIN

Bucharin, a close friend and companion of Lenin, is the editor of *Pravda*, the party organ in Moscow. I learned that he, too, had been in America for two or three months previous to the overthrow of the Czar, and had hurried back when this news reached him. He is a small figure, always hurrying somewhere, with a book under his arm. One meets him in the Theater Square in the morning, in Soviet Square a few hours later, at the Kremlin still later, and in the evening at the extreme opposite end of the city. There is a saying about him, "One can never tell where he will turn up next. He is always on the move." And yet he always has time for a kindly word or question or greeting. He is a student of history and quotes freely, from memory, all the Russian and many European writers.

GEORGE MELCHOIR

George Melchoir is president of the Moscow Central Federation of All-Russian Professional Alliances. He worked for a long time at Bayonne, New Jersey, but like many others returned to Russia after the overthrow of the Czar. He took an active part in organizing the taking of Moscow in the early days of the Bolshevist uprising.

Melchoir has been a working man all his life, and is extremely intelligent. The position which he holds demands a great deal of technical knowledge, as well as executive ability, and every one agreed that he was thoroughly qualified for his post. I had a long talk with him. He was enthusiastic about the future of Russia. It would be built up, he said, by the various unions and peasant organizations.

He is probably thirty-five years of age, of medium height, with a bulky figure, full of vigor and enthusiasm.

PETERS

In the early days of the revolution Peters was chief of the Internal Defense of Petrograd. American newspapers said of him that "his fingers were cramped from writing death warrants." I asked him how many death warrants he had signed and he told me three hundred in all. He expressed regret that he had been looked upon in other countries as a murderer, and said it was unfortunate that those people did not understand the conditions that surrounded Russia while in the throes of a revolution. He insisted that the warrants he had signed had been necessary in the interest of the country as a whole, and that they had been signed only after investigation and a trial of the individuals, and that in no case had there been an execution to gratify the personal revenge of any one.

He is a Lett, very young, perhaps between twenty-eight and thirty years old, short and stocky, with a mass of black hair combed straight back. He lived in England for a number of years, and speaks the English language easily and fluently.

BORIS REINSTEIN

As a former resident of Buffalo, New York, and member of the American Socialist Labor Party, Boris Reinstein returned to Russia after the overthrow of the Czar. He was for some time an assistant in the Foreign Office; later a lecturer in a military school, and is now an official lecturer in the large college for training writers and speakers in Moscow. This school was running full blast while I was there. Classes number from seventy-five to one hundred each. Pupils are elected by various Soviet organizations over the country, and at the end of six months' training are returned to their various communities and others are sent into their places. The Government supports all these pupils while they are in training.

Reinstein is an excellent speaker and a tireless worker, and is one of the kindest and most conscientious men I have ever met. He is certainly not the "wild-eyed agitator" he has been pictured in the American press. He has given valuable service to the revolution, though he has lost twenty-five pounds in doing so.

"BILL" SHATOFF

"Bill" Shatoff, described by American papers as "the well-known anarchist," is one of the officials of the Soviet Army. When I was in Petrograd he was the commander of the Petrograd front. He is a big jolly Russian Jew, and certainly does not look any the worse for his participation in Soviet warfare, nor for the stinted rations he has shared with his men.

CHILDREN OF THE SOVIET SCHOOL AT DIETSKOE SELO

Formerly Tsarskoe Selo, the residence of the Czar

CHAPTER IX
WOMEN AND CHILDREN

The Education of the children occupies as important a place in the administration of the Soviet Government as the maintenance of the Red Army. The Budget for education and child welfare is unstinted, and at every turn one encounters evidence of actual accomplishment in the interest of the growing generation. "First we must defend the workers' state against its enemies," said a Commissar to me, "then we must prepare the coming generation to carry on and develop the state won for them by the Red Army."

In the two years of the revolution 10,000 new schools had been opened. There were but few children in Soviet Russia who are not attending classes in grades from kindergarten to high school. I saw few children idling indoors or out during school hours, nor did I see any at work in the factories. They troop out from the schools in great bands into the parks at recess hour. Teachers complained to me of the lack of text-books, due to the scarcity of paper. They resented bitterly, too, the necessity of assembling their charges in cold class-rooms.

But in spite of meagre facilities, every one connected with the government worked hard to make every possible provision for the care and protection of the children. The government was feeding 359,000 children daily in the schools in Moscow, and 200,000 in Petrograd. The most nourishing food obtainable was requisitioned for the children. Milk, butter and eggs went first to hospitals and to the school restaurants, where the children were provided with food free. Only when there was an extra supply were healthy adults permitted to purchase these foods.

I used to watch the children, happy, robust little folk, going from their class-rooms in great crowds to the restaurants, where they sat in rows at the long tables. The noon recess lasted for two hours—one hour for eating and one for play. The children were chaperoned by their teachers, of whom there were two for each roomful of pupils. One looked after the mental studies, while the other directed their physical training.

The children of kindergarten age were called for in the mornings by their teachers, and were brought home by them at about four o'clock in the afternoon. At least ninety-five percent of the teachers were women, and they had all received special training for their profession.

The Soviet law prohibits the employment of children under sixteen years, except in cases of greatest necessity. Child labor under fourteen is forbidden. Children between fourteen and eighteen permitted to enter certain industries are not allowed to work more than four hours a day; between sixteen and eighteen they may work not more than six hours daily, and all must spend two hours in school.

With much of the work of preparing meals and the care of children of school age taken away from them, the women of Russia were enjoying a new freedom. They had found themselves suddenly with time to work away from home. They rushed into industry and the professions and set to work with an ardor and enthusiasm that has done much to establish the Soviet system.

Women conductors were employed on the street-cars in all the cities in the daytime, men being employed only at night. Women police also were employed, and no one seemed to think this extraordinary.

Housekeepers were accorded the same right to vote as factory workers. If a married woman had a desire to work elsewhere than in her home she did so, and took her meals with her husband and friends in a Soviet restaurant. Women shared in the discussions in the Soviet, and were elected to offices. Far from being "nationalized," women were accorded the same respect and treatment as men.

The right of inheritance has been abolished, although dependents such as minors unable to work, or invalids, are supported out of the property of the deceased former owner, and no discrimination is made against children born out of wedlock.

The government recognizes only civil marriages, but an additional religious ceremony is optional with the contracting parties and is not restricted in any way by the government. An oral or written statement of the parties desiring to contract the marriage is required by the nearest Department of Registration. Boys under eighteen and girls under sixteen are prohibited from marrying, and the laws of consanguinity in force in other countries are observed in Russia also. Births must be registered in the Department of Registration nearest the mother's residence, and children born out of wedlock have the same status as those born of a registered union.

Divorces are granted on the petition of either or both parties. When the petition is mutual the persons are obliged to state what surnames the children of the marriage are expected to bear in future. In case only one party petitions, the surname of the children and the responsibility for maintenance are decided by the judge.

In Moscow I visited a lying-in hospital under the Division of Motherhood and Infants, of the Department of Social Welfare. This was one of many similar institutions this department had established in all the large and many of the small cities. Here the working women receive care and nourishment without cost for several weeks before and after child-birth. They have the best food and medical treatment obtainable, and are paid their full wages during the time they are out of their accustomed employment. In connection with this hospital in Moscow, which was established in an imposing white stone structure formerly an *élite* finishing school where the daughters of the rich learned French and the gentle arts, there was a training college where five hundred young women, chosen by various trade and peasant organizations throughout the country, were attending a six months' course of lectures and practical demonstrations on obstetrics and the care of children. Already three classes of five hundred each had been graduated and sent back to their respective communities to apply their experience and to train others.

Moving pictures were shown daily, portraying to the mothers the best methods of bathing, dressing, and caring for their infants, and these were supplemented with lectures. Older children of working mothers were cared for during the day in government nurseries, where they were given the best possible care and attention.

The following is a table showing the record of the accomplishments in this department in the year 1919.

MATERNITY AND CHILD WELFARE INSTITUTIONS

In Moscow and the principal government towns, from returns received in October, 1918, and July, 1919

CITIES	Asylums for Newborn Children		Asylums for Children From 1 to 3		Crèches		Ambulatoriums for Newborn Children Consultations		Milk Kitchens		Asylums for Mothers with Newborn Children	
	1918	1919	1918	1919	1918	1919	1918	1919	1918	1919	1918	1919
Moscow	1	2	2	6	4	26	8	17	8	10	1	3
Yaroslav	1	1	..	..	1	3	..	2	..	1	..	..
Kostroma	1	2	..	1	2	2	..	2	..	1	..	1
Ivanov-na-Voznesensk		1	..	1	2	3	..	..	..	2	..	..
Tula	1	1	..	1	..	1	..	..	..	..	..	..
Saratov	1	1	..	1	..	..	3	4	3	4	..	1
Voronezh	1	1	..	1	..	..	1	1	1	1	1	2
Tver	1	8	..	6	3	6	..	2	..	..	..	..
Tambov	1	9	..	7	2	2	1	1	1	1	..	..
Minsk	1	2	..	1	..	2	1	2	1	2	..	..
Kaluga	1	1	..	4	2	6	..	1	..	1	..	..
Vitebsk	1	1	..	1	..	..	1	2	1	2	..	..
Tomsk	1	1	..	1	..	..	1	4	..	4	..	..
TOTAL	12	31	2	31	16	51	16	38	15	29	2	7

More than 2,500 libraries had been established throughout the country since the revolution. All the larger towns have their high schools, technical schools, and musical conservatories.

As every able-bodied adult must work in Soviet Russia, I wondered who went to the advanced technical schools. Each local Soviet elected its group of students to attend schools for special training for terms varying from three to six months. At the end of the training the students returned to their communities to teach, and a new group was sent for similar training. The schools were free; the students were furnished with food, clothing, living quarters and books, and were provided with tickets for theatres, concerts and other entertainments. All students were granted loans, to be used for spending money while in school, if they preferred to purchase their own clothing and other necessaries. In Moscow the average loan was 1,200 rubles, varying according to the rise or fall of the ruble's value.

Throughout the country homes for the aged had been established where men over sixty and women over fifty were cared for by the government, provided they did not have children or relatives who wished to keep them in their own homes. In the latter case they were given adequate pensions.

MRS. LENIN VISITING A SOVIET SCHOOL

The children, under the supervision of their teacher, are busy in the garden.

I found less of the "institution" atmosphere in these homes than in those I have seen in other countries. Books, pictures, a meeting-room, and dining-room, and a general atmosphere of comfort and freedom seemed to make the elderly people content and happy. They are not considered "paupers" or "charges on the state," but human beings who have contributed their service to society and are entitled to all the peace and comfort society can give them.

I have dwelt upon the organization and spirit of the Red Army and upon the education and care of the children more than upon anything else, because these are the things that made the strongest impression upon me during my stay in Soviet Russia. They stand out above all else in the memory of weeks crowded with a multitude of rapid and various observations. The soldiers and the children come first in the consideration of the government. Here the greatest ingenuity and energy have been applied, and here the best results are evident. It has been the purpose of the Soviet leaders to make the first line of defense—the army—unconquerable. Government officials claim they have succeeded in this, and point to the map as evidence. The children, they say, are the strategical reserves of the communist state. They are aiming to keep them healthy in body, despite the privations imposed by the blockade, and to develop them mentally and physically to carry on the future state. No one can deny the large measure of success realized.

CHAPTER X

GOVERNMENT INDUSTRY AND AGRICULTURE

THE SOVIET STATE

The All-Russian Congress of Soviets is composed of representatives of urban Soviets, one delegate for 25,000 voters, and of rural Soviets, one delegate for 125,000 inhabitants. This Congress is convoked at least twice a year. There had already been six meetings. The Congress elects an All-Russian Central Executive Committee of not more than two hundred members, which is the supreme power of the republic, in all periods between convocations of the Congress. It directs in a general way the activities of the Workers' and Peasants' Government, considers and enacts all measures or proposals introduced by the Soviet of Peoples' Commissars, convokes the Congress of Soviets, and forms a Council of People's Commissars. This council in turn is entrusted with the general management of the affairs of the republic and in this capacity issues decrees, resolutions and orders, notifying the Central Executive Committee immediately of all such orders or decrees.

There are seventeen of these Commissars, (1) Foreign Affairs, (2) Army, (3) Navy, (4) Interior, (5) Justice, (6) Labor, (7) Social Welfare, (8) Education, (9) Post and Telegraph, (10) National Affairs, (11) Finances, (12) Ways of Communication, (13) Agriculture, (14) Commerce and Industry, (15) National Supplies, (16) Supreme Soviet of National Economy, (17) Public Health. Each Commissar has a collegium, or committee, the members of which are appointed by the Council of People's Commissars, of which body Lenin is the president.

These committees act as the administrators of the nation, dealing with ratification and amendments to the constitution; the general interior and foreign policy of the republic; boundaries; the admission or secessions of new members; the establishing or changing of weights, measures, or money denominations; declarations of war or peace treaties; loans, commercial agreements or treaties; taxes; military affairs; legislation and judicial procedure; civil and criminal procedure; and citizenship.

Local affairs are administered by local Soviets, in the following order: Rural Soviets, of ten or less than ten members, send one delegate to the rural congress, which in turn sends one delegate for each ten of its members to the County Soviet Congress. This County Soviet Congress sends one delegate for each 1,000 inhabitants (though not more than three hundred in all may be sent) to the Provincial

Soviet Congress, which is made up of representatives of both urban and rural Soviets. The Provincial Soviet Congress sends from its body one representative for 10,000 inhabitants of the rural districts, and one for each 2,000 voters in the city, to the Regional Soviet Congress. This Congress sends one delegate for each 125,000 inhabitants to the All-Russian Congress of Soviets.

All these Congresses of Soviets elect their own executive committees for handling local affairs, but in small rural districts questions are decided at general meetings of the voters whenever possible. The functions of the local Congresses of Soviets and deputies are given thus in the Constitution: To carry out all orders of the respective higher organs of the Soviet Power; to take all steps for raising the cultural and economic standard of the given territory; to decide all questions of local importance within their respective territories; and to coordinate all Soviet activity in their respective territories.

Roughly speaking, the Supreme Council of National Economy, which is established under the Council of the People's Commissars, deals with the organization and distribution of production. It coordinates the activities of the federal and the local Soviets, and has the right of confiscation, requisition, or compulsory syndication of various branches of industry and commerce; it determines the amount of raw materials and fuel needed, obtains and distributes them, and organizes and supplies the rural economy. It works in close and constant touch with the All-Russian Professional Alliances, and under its direction the latter constantly regulates the wage scales in accordance with the rise and fall of prices of commodities. When I was in Moscow the average wage paid was 3,000 rubles per month, and in Petrograd 3,500. A member of the Council of People's Commissars received 4,500 per month, out of which he had to pay rent and buy food and clothing. Lenin, as president, received the same amount, which was equivalent to about $180 in American money.

All men and women of the republic belonging to the following classes are allowed to vote after their eighteenth year: Individuals doing productive or useful work; all persons engaged in housekeeping which enables others to do productive work; peasants who employ no help in agricultural labor; soldiers of the army and sailors of the navy; citizens who are incapacited for work; and foreigners who live in and are working for the republic.

Suffrage and candidacy are denied to persons who employ labor in order to obtain profits; persons who live on an income, such as interest from capital, receipts from property, etc.; private merchants, trade or commercial brokers; monks and clergy of all denominations;[1] employees and agents of the former police, gendarmes, or secret service; persons under legal guardianship, or who have been declared by law as demented or mentally deficient; and persons who have been deprived of their rights of citizenship by a Soviet, for selfish or dishonorable offences for the term fixed by the Soviet.

The Church has been separated from the State and the School from the Church,

[1] There have been some modifications of this regulation recently. I have heard since my return to America that clergymen are given the right to vote provided they are supported by the workers and not from endowments.

but the right of religious or anti-religious propaganda is accorded to every citizen. The government press has been freed from all dependence upon capital in the form of advertising, and all the technical and material means for publication, as well as for the publication of books and pamphlets are free. Furnished halls, with heating and lighting free, are given to the poorest peasantry for meeting-places.

LAND NATIONALIZATION

The brief Land Decree of November 7, 1917, was replaced in September, 1918, by "The Fundamental Law of Socialization of the Land," which has already been enforced throughout the country except in the cases of land owned by peasants and worked by the owner and his family. This land decree has been enforced gradually, and perhaps less completely than any other of the Soviet decrees, first because the energies of the Government were diverted to a war of defence, and secondly, because the land question would naturally take the longest to settle even in times of peace.

The land decree provides that all property rights in land, minerals, oil, gas, peat, medicinal springs, waters, timber and other natural resources be abolished and the land given to the use of the entire laboring population, without open or secret compensation to former owners. The right to use this land belongs to those who till it by their own labor, and is not restricted by sex, religion, nationality, or foreign citizenship. Under-surface deposits, timber, etc., are at the disposal of the Soviet powers, local or federal, and all live stock and agricultural implements are to be taken over without indemnification by the land departments of the Soviets. Infants, or minors, cripples, invalids, or aged persons who would be deprived of their means of subsistence by the enforcement of this decree are pensioned either for life or until they attain their majority. Minors are given the same pension as soldiers.

Land may be used for cultural and educational purposes; for agricultural purposes, communities, associations, village organizations, individuals and families; and for industrial, commercial and transportation enterprises under the control of the Soviet power. It is given to those who wish to work it for themselves, to local agricultural workers whose plots are now too small, or who have been employed by land owners, and to immigrants who come from towns or cities in order to work on the land.

When the land was turned over to the peasants each one seized the opportunity to establish his own little homestead. Since that time the peasants have discovered the benefits of cooperative agricultural production, and have established their own agricultural communes all over the country.

ONE OF THE MANY TRAINS CIRCULATING SOVIET PROPAGANDA
THROUGHOUT RUSSIA

In the Orel Government there were 391 of these communes, covering 39,000 dessiatins,[2] with a population of 29,000 people. In the province of Moghilev there were 225, with more than 11,000 people and 40,000 dessiatins of land. In the Vitebsk government there were 214, covering 60,000 dessiatins of land with a population of 60,000. In the province of Novgorod there were 72, with 11,376 inhabitants and 22,253 dessiatins. In Kaluga 150, with 6,500 inhabitants, covering 12,000 dessiatins. Officials estimated that this number would be doubled before the end of 1919. In the Petrograd Government 830 communes were organized, with 17,000 dessiatins and 15,313 inhabitants, all of whom were laborers. In Tula there were 78, with 5,465 workers, and 8,554 dessiatins of land.

LABOR LAWS

The Soviet Russian Code of Labor Laws passed by the Russian Central Executive Committee in 1919 covers the whole field of Russian labor activities. To workers in other countries some of the provisions will appear drastic, but it must be remembered that Russia is still an armed camp and that the war has disorganized industry, transportation and almost every other form of endeavor. I was informed that every effort was being made under these laws to coordinate the productive forces of the country with a view to securing the highest possible production for the pressing needs of the Russian people. When the war stops, as it no doubt will in the immediate future, Soviet Russia will be faced with the problem of diverting into productive channels its three million soldiers, as well as other millions now engaged directly or indirectly in the war. Just as we had our "Work or Fight" measures in this country for the purpose of utilizing the nation's human energy in a profitable way in time of stress, so in Soviet Russia every effort is being made to place the workers where the greatest results to the nation as a whole will accrue.

In connection with the passage of these labor laws, it must be borne in mind that the working people in Soviet Russia enjoy much more control at the present time than do the same class of people in possibly any other country. One must take into consideration the fact that these laws were initiated by the unions themselves or their representatives, who shared jointly with the political side of the Government the responsibility for maintaining the new order. Many of the former so-called bourgeoisie of the old regime, I was informed, have spent the past two years doing nothing but live by speculation and they stir up trouble on the slightest pretext against the new Government. It was primarily to reach recalcitrants of this character that the compulsory provisions were inserted in the code. The result of the passage of these laws did not, so far as I could judge, diminish the enthusiasm of the Russian workers for the new order, but on the other hand their energy seems to have been stimulated, no doubt because they were beginning to feel that through their various organizations this step had been taken for the express purpose of forcing into production every man and woman in the country capable of producing and helping to reconstruct Russia.

Article I of the code deals with compulsory labor. It provides that all citizens of the Soviet Republic, with the following exceptions, are subject to compulsory

---

[2] A dessiatin is approximately 2.7 acres.

labor:

First, persons under sixteen years of age; second, all persons over fifty years of age; third, persons who have become incapacitated by injury or illness; fourth, women for a period of eight weeks before and eight weeks after confinement.

All students are subject to compulsory labor at the schools. Labor conditions in all establishments, Soviet, nationalized, public and private, are regulated by tariff rules drafted by the trade unions in agreement with the directors or owners of establishments and enterprises and approved by the people's commissariat of labor.

Article II, entitled "The Right to Work," provides that all citizens able to work have the right to employment at their vocations and remuneration fixed for such class of work. The district exchange bureaus of the Department of Labor Distribution, in agreement with respective unions, assign individual wage earners or groups of them to work at other trades if there is no demand for labor at the vocation of the persons in question. All persons of the female sex and those of the male sex under eighteen years of age have no right to work at night or in those industries in which the conditions of labor are especially hard or dangerous.

Article III, provides for the methods of labor distribution. Any wage earner who is not engaged on work at his vocation shall register at the Local Department of Labor Distribution as unemployed. An unemployed person has no right to refuse an offer of work at his vocation, providing the working conditions conform with the standards fixed by the respective tariff regulations, or, in the absence of the same, by the trades unions. An unemployed person who is offered work outside his vocation shall be obliged to accept it on the understanding, if he so wishes, that this be only until he receives work at his vocation.

Article V, makes provision for the transfer of a wage earner to other work within the enterprise, establishment or institution where he is employed. His transfer may be ordered by the managing authorities of said enterprise, establishment or institution. The decision of the Department of Labor in the matter of a transfer of labor may be appealed from under the law by the interested parties to the District Department of Labor or to the People's Commissariat of Labor, whose decision of the matter in dispute is final. In case of urgent public work the Department of Labor, in agreement with the respective professional unions, may order the transfer of a whole group of wage earners from the organization where they are employed to another situated in the same or a different locality. This is done, provided a sufficient number of volunteers for such work cannot be found.

Under Article VI, which covers remuneration of labor, the law provides that in working out tariff rates and determining the standard rates of remuneration all wage earners of a trade shall be divided into groups of skill, and a definite standard of remuneration shall be fixed for each group. In determining the standard of remuneration for each category, consideration must be given to the kind of labor, the danger of the conditions under which the work is performed, the complexity and accuracy of the work. Remuneration for piece-work is computed by dividing the daily tariff rate by the number of pieces constituting the production standard.

Remuneration for overtime work shall not exceed time and a half. During illness of a wage earner the remuneration due him shall be paid as a subsidy from the hospital fund. The unemployed receive a subsidy out of the funds for unemployed.

Under Article VII, which deals with working hours, provision is made that the duration of a normal working day must in no case exceed eight hours for day work and seven hours for night work, and that the duration of a normal day, first, for persons under eighteen years of age, and second, for persons working in especially hard or health-endangering branches of industry, must not exceed six hours. In case the nature of the work is such that it requires a working day in excess of the normal, two or more shifts shall be engaged. Except in extreme cases work in excess of the normal hours, or what is usually called overtime work, is not permitted. No females and no males under eighteen years of age may do any overtime work, and the time spent by those on such work in the course of two consecutive days must not exceed four hours. All wage earners must be allowed a weekly uninterrupted rest of not less than forty-two hours, and on the eve of rest days the normal working day is reduced by two hours. Every wage earner who has worked without interruption not less than six months shall be entitled to leave of absence for two weeks, and every wage earner who has worked without interruption not less than a year shall be entitled to leave of absence for not less than one month with full pay.

Article VIII deals with methods to insure efficiency of labor. The standard output for wage earners of each trade and group is fixed by valuation commissions of the respective trades unions. This article provides that a wage earner systematically producing less than the fixed standard may be transferred by the decision of the proper valuation commission to other work in the same group and category, or to a lower group or category with a corresponding reduction of wages. However, appeal can be taken from this provision of the law as well as all other provisions in the code.

Article IX provides for protection of life, health and labor of persons engaged in any economic activity, and the carrying out of this part of the law is entrusted to labor inspectors, technical inspectors and the representatives of sanitary inspection. The labor inspection is under the jurisdiction of the People's Commissariat of Labor and its local branches, which are the Departments of Labor, and is composed of labor inspectors, elected by the councils of professional unions. The inspectors are compelled under the law to visit at any time of the day or night all the industrial enterprises of their district and all places where work is carried on, as well as places provided for the workmen by the enterprises, such as rooming-houses, asylums, baths, etc., and to assist the trades unions and works committee in their efforts to ameliorate in individual enterprises as well as in branches of industry.

This brief outline of the Code of Labor Laws, the full text of which will be found in the appendix, shows how thoroughly the new régime in Russia has gone into the question of organizing the labor power of the country for production on the highest scale. I was told over and over again by various officials of the labor organizations of Soviet Russia and the Government officials as well, that what they were interested in above all else at the present time was the organization of labor along lines that would insure sufficient production of essential commodities to meet the needs of all the people under Soviet rule.

TRANSPORTATION

Before the war there were in Russia 37,000 railway locomotives. At the end of the war 13,000 were left. Of these, at the time of the Brest Litovsk treaty, thirty-five percent were disabled. In the spring of 1919 the total number of disabled locomotives amounted to fifty percent. Since that time there has been some improvement, and last August only forty-seven percent of them were disabled. There is a great demand for locomotives. Russia could use to advantage the entire product of the United States for the next six years. Approximately the same conditions prevail with reference to cars.

Practically the whole transportation system was given over to the movement of troops and army supplies. In certain sections of the country there was a surplus of grain, but no facilities to transport it to the cities.

On the last stage of the journey to Moscow I had a vivid glimpse into the transportation problem of Soviet Russia. Two or three hours out of Smolensk we stopped at a small way station and hooked on seventeen cars loaded with wood intended to relieve the critical fuel shortage in Moscow. After five or six hours' journey, with only brief stops, the train made a prolonged halt. I got out to learn the cause of the delay. The cars loaded with wood had been uncoupled from the train and men were busy throwing the billets into the field by the track. The station was crowded with soldiers. Word had been received to rush reinforcements southward to meet the advance of Denikin. These cars were needed to carry the troops.

"What about the wood?" I asked, "Isn't it needed in Moscow?"

"Yes," was the reply. "The nights are getting very cold in Moscow. But Moscow must wait. The army comes first."

Such incidents were happening daily, hourly, no doubt, all over Russia. Always, they complained, the necessities of the war and the mobilization hampered the productive enterprises of the nation.

INDUSTRY

While I was in Moscow the Government received a report from the Supreme Council of National Economy to the effect that war industry was progressing at full speed and producing sufficient supplies and ammunitions for the army. In addition the departments of building materials, fur, leather, fuel, metal, chemicals, and trade, had been organized. There were fifty-one factories in the building material branch alone, capable of producing 121,500,000 bricks, 2,000,000 poods of cement, 870,000 poods of lime, and 510,000 poods of tiles. The tanneries were running on the basis of 240,800 poods annually. The department of forests had obtained a contract for twenty percent of the fuel demand, in the Moscow Government alone. There were sixty-eight saw mills and 128 planing mills running on full time. All paper factories were working. The chemical department controls the paper, china, and chemical production. The trade department supervised 175,000 workers and had its own art industry museum.

The Government is planning the construction of enormous power systems, one of which will be the largest in the world. They will also utilize the water falls for great hydraulic power stations, all of which would require great amounts of machinery from America.

CANALS

The Volga and Don canal will connect the Black and Caspian Seas and the Volga river with the Baltic Sea. Canal Dredges are needed to build these.

RAW MATERIALS

There are at present in warehouses in Russia 200,000 tons of flax, the present market price of which, in London, is over $1,000 per ton. There are also 100,000 tons of hemp. There is gold, timber, and ninety percent of the world's supply of platinum.

Many factories will be erected, great rolling mills, steel mills, etc. There is no doubt but that Russia will eventually be able to produce everything it needs. The country is thoroughly stocked with all kinds of mineral products and it is merely a matter of time before it will be entirely independent. It struck me that in the meantime the American business men are missing a wonderful opportunity in these ready markets for their machinery and equipment. Russia will be, in the course of a very few years, a very strong competitor, whereas now it offers a vast market.

CHAPTER XI
PROPAGANDA

On my way into Red Russia the train on which I was travelling passed, between Rejistza and Novo-Sokoliev, a train of ten or twelve cars, the sides of which were covered with huge, multi-colored placards. It was the "Lenin Train" used for carrying propaganda literature all over the republic. When I saw it, it was on a tour of the country behind the Western Front.

The train was decorated with great paintings in bright colors and with revolutionary inscriptions. In one of the cars was a moving picture apparatus and screen; another was fitted up as a book shop; and a third as a telegraph station which posted the latest news bulletins at every station, and circulated news from the front and from the rest of the world. The train carried representatives from government departments and a staff of speakers and lecturers.

It had been in constant service for about two months, during which time it travelled through the districts of Pskov, Vitebsk, Lettonia, White Russia, Lithuania, and Kharkov, covering some 3,590 versts. In all the stations and towns through which it passed, leaflets, pamphlets and books were distributed. Meetings were arranged and lectures given, and the Commissary representatives visited the Soviet institutions offering suggestions and aid. Workers and peasants assembled about the train and listened to speeches made from the roofs of cars and gathered bundles of literature to be distributed in the villages and workshops. They told of their difficulties to the speakers and asked them for their advice.

In America I had always heard so much about the illiteracy of the Russian peasants that I wondered what use quantities of reading matter would be to them. I discovered that illiteracy was not nearly so general as popularly supposed, and was decreasing rapidly under the government's energetic educational program. In every community there is at least one who can read and write. Russians live in villages everywhere; even on the plains or steppes such a thing as an isolated farmhouse or workman's cottage is rare. The farmer may, and often does, have to go some distance to work his land, but his home is always among other homes. When literatures arrives those who can, read aloud. The others gather around the reader to listen. Long discussions, so dearly loved by the Russians, follow.

The "Lenin Train" was preceded by telegraphic announcements of its coming, so there was a crowd to meet it at every station. Sometimes the reception was very ceremonious. At Rejistza, where it arrived at night, it was met with banners, music and torches. At a tiny station, Malinooka, a crowd of peasants from the nearby villages was waiting to receive their literature and "to hear directly from the seat of their government." I learned that five more similar trains were being prepared to be put on the Volga and its tributaries, and motor-trucks to be sent into the sections where neither railways nor waterways entered. One was to be called "The October Revolution," another "The Communist," and a third "The Red Army." The others were not yet named. Boats too were used for that purpose.

It was easy to understand why these people, beset on all sides, were carrying on propaganda to defend their country. But I found that their propaganda did not end with this defensive material. By far the greater proportion of it was what might be called cultural. It was intended not only to waken the people to a realization that their own lives were threatened, but to teach them that they were a part of the great world that lay outside their own land. The art, the music, the literature and the science of the world was brought to them in simple form so that they could comprehend it and be stimulated to further reading and study. Whatever else the Russians may be they are not materialistic. I found them more eager for news and knowledge than for food, of which they got so little. Whatever news is obtained from the outside world is disseminated at once, by telegraph and bulletins, to all parts of the country.

At the town of Praele a Bolshevist soldier said to me with a twinkle in his eye, "You have a great country in America."

"Why do you think it a great country?" I asked.

"They are shooting negroes in Chicago and Washington now," was his answer; "and that's the country that talks about Soviet Russia being barbarous."

Naturally I was interested in the confirmation or refutation of the reports I had heard, that the Bolsheviki intend to spread their propaganda all over the world. Soviet officials talked frankly to me about prisoners and propaganda. They liked to take prisoners, they said. They only wished they had more food so that they could afford to take more of them. They didn't want them to starve. They would like to take a million prisoners a day if they had enough food and paper. "After all," they said, "our war is primarily a war of education."

At many points along the battlefronts I saw great banners stretched between posts, with letters large enough to be read a hundred yards away, telling the other side what the war was about. One, which I had translated for me on the Lettish front, read, "The Germans are marching on Riga. German soldiers are helping you to destroy the working class republic in Russia. If you want to defend Lettland go back and drive the Germans out of Riga." The Russians placed great reliance on this battlefront propaganda. I found evidence in the Lettish ranks of the effectiveness of these tactics.

In striking contrast to the enthusiasm of the Soviet officials for this propaganda at the fighting front, and their reliance upon it to achieve important military results, was their seeming indifference to propaganda abroad. They were anxious enough that the case for the Russian revolution and the Soviet Government should be presented to the people of other countries, but they displayed none of that eager confidence in their ability to stir revolution abroad with which they are commonly credited. They believed that by means of propaganda they could break the morale of any army brought against them; but they did not pretend to be able to subvert remote governments. They were amused by the fear of Bolshevik propaganda displayed in the foreign press. They were not inclined to rate their powers so highly. "To be sure," they told me, "we are internationalists and revolutionists, but if other countries are not ready for revolution how can we stimulate it? That is not our job. We have had our revolution in Russia and we must bend all our energies to preserve it. The workers in other countries must take care of their own affairs."

"RED TERROR"

Execution of a Red Guard on an English gunboat in Lake Onega, Russia, in the presence of English and American Officers

They were willing to give guarantees that the Soviet Government would not engage in revolutionary propaganda abroad. They told me that they had repeatedly assured foreign journalists and agents that their governments could take any measures they saw fit to protect themselves against Russian propaganda.

Of propaganda in Russia itself there is plenty. I have already described the propaganda among prisoners of war, and of its effect upon the English prisoners in Moscow. I have no doubt the same "torture" was administered to Americans in Siberia. I saw, in an American magazine, a statement of a Canadian soldier that he and many of his comrades had been entirely converted to the doctrines of Bolshevism, but he attributed his conversion to actual experiences and to the things he saw rather than to anything he had read or been told. It occurs to an unprejudiced observer who has been in Soviet Russia that the nations that feared the contagion of Bolshevist propaganda took the worst possible way of avoiding it when they sent their young soldiers into a land full of propaganda explaining and upholding the new order established there.

CHAPTER XII
COMING OUT OF SOVIET RUSSIA

I was checked and guarded out of Red Russia in the same manner in which I had been checked and guarded into it. When I was ready to leave Petrograd, early in October, Zinovieff delegated as my guard and guide a short, stocky Esthonian, Isaac Mikkal. As Grafman had reminded me of Larkin, so Mikkal reminded me of Tom Hickey, the famous Texas socialist. He appeared rather pleased at my calling him "Hickey" which I did, throughout the journey.

We left Petrograd at eleven o'clock at night, and arrived at Pskov the next morning at eight, where we had to remain until five in the evening before we could get a train for Rejistza, which we reached at six the following day. Here the division commandant stamped our papers and sent us on to Velikie Luki to the headquarters of the army command.

"Hickey" had turned out to be a less aggressive and efficient guide than Larkin, and as he could give me little information about either the country we were passing through or the events that were taking place, I longed often for my old friend whom I had left at Moscow weeks before. With our papers stamped at Velikie Luki, we were allowed to go on to the front without going through Smolensk, and I asked the commandant to give me a guide who understood that part of the Western Front, so that I could proceed more swiftly. He granted this request, but said that "Hickey" must also be of the party, since he had been charged at Petrograd with my safe delivery and must make his report on his return to that city. After a brief telephone conversation, in Russian, the commandant informed me that another guide would appear in less than a half hour. We had dinner and waited calmly. At the end of the stipulated time my guide entered, and to my surprise and pleasure it was "Larkin."

He stopped short, looked at me a moment, raised his hands to his head and brushed off his cap which fell to the floor. "God love a duck, is it you? They told me there was a journalist here who wanted to go to the front but if I had known it was you I would have said I was laid up with cholera."

I introduced my two guides and we went to the station, only to find that the train we had expected to take at eleven that night would not go before five the next morning. There was nothing to do but climb in one of the coaches, but since the train was already full of soldiers, talking, singing, and smoking, there was but little sleep for me that night.

At five in the morning we started—on time at last. The conductor informed me that we would reach Rejistza at five in the afternoon, but we did not arrive until four in the morning. I endeavored to learn from both "Larkin" and "Hickey" the real reason for the delay, but they told me to "forget it. A few hours' delay makes no difference to you, one way or the other." At last "Larkin" must have grown very weary of my importunities. At any rate he said, "Please remember you are in Russia and that we are at war. All trains are soldier trains. They must stop to take on soldiers and to let soldiers off. They must stop to make repairs. They must stop for many reasons. Don't imagine you are in America, on an express train. Some time when the war is over trains will run on time, but now,—well stop kicking." I stopped.

In Rejistza we learned that we must wait until four P.M. for a train going to the Dvinsk front. In the division commandant's office we found two foreigners who had come across the front the night before. They were on the way to Moscow, and were being checked in as I had been. The commandant asked "Larkin," whom he knew quite well, if he would take them to Velikie Luki; and on "Larkin's" saying that he had been entrusted with the task of seeing me to the front, the commandant told him that "Hickey" could see me through. I was sorry to lose "Larkin," but there was nothing else to be done, and we parted with a cordial wish that we might meet again under more favorable circumstances. "But, God love a duck,—I hope you stay out of Russia until peace comes," were his last words to me.

When "Hickey" and I finally reached Dvinsk the Poles were shelling the town. The soldier train on which I was traveling stopped two miles outside the city and the soldiers detrained and began marching into Dvinsk to reinforce their comrades. I did not wish to go through Dvinsk. One experience under shell-fire had been sufficiently shocking to my nervous system, and it wasn't my war at any rate. I protested to "Hickey" that he had been instructed to see me *safely* across the front, and demanded that he take me to some other point where I could cross. He told me that the papers read that I was to pass through the Dvinsk front. I said that, papers to the contrary notwithstanding, I refused to cross at Dvinsk. Poor "Hickey" crossed to an officer and held a discussion, during which he made a few notes. At the conclusion of their talk he returned to me "If you *won't* go this way," he told me, "we will have to go back on this train seventy-five versts and then drive ten versts across country to the thirty-second division command to get your papers amended. Then you'll have to return to the same station, wait for a train, ride forty versts, get off and drive twenty-two versts across country to the brigade command of this division, and then from there we will have to drive twenty versts more to the Soviet outposts, where you can get into the neutral zone and start for the Lettish outposts seventeen versts away."

All my former desire for speedy travel and short cuts seemed to have evaporated. I yielded meekly to this decree and was, I believe, fairly patient during the two days it took us to carry out this long program. When we finally arrived at the Soviet front I was told to start down the road and walk seventeen versts, which would bring me into Lettish territory. Again my suitcase was heavy, or rather it was still heavy, and I protested that I could not walk so far and carry it. But no vehicles were available in that part of the country. My officer informant pointed to a village two or three versts away, across a field, and said: "When you get to that village you may be able to hire a hay-rick."

Even that comparatively short walk did not appear attractive, but at this particular moment there came around a bend in the road an old Russian driving a familiar hay-rick. He readily consented to take me to the village, and after saying farewell to "Hickey," and enjoining him to "keep smiling," my aged saviour and I set out on our journey. A half hour later, in the village, I tried my best, with my still limited Russian vocabulary, to procure another hay-rick to drive me the fourteen versts remaining between me and the Lettish front. Out of the crowd of villagers that surrounded me there emerged a Lettish boy of perhaps fifteen years, who told me in German that he would take me across. When the villagers understood what I wanted, the peasant women insisted that I must have food before starting. I was taken into one of the dingy little homes, where I was served with good rye bread, butter, milk, and eggs, which I ate greedily, I am afraid, for I was very hungry. Not even the thousands of flies that I had to brush away before I could take a bite prevented my enjoyment of this food.

At seven in the evening my boy rescuer and I reached the Lettish front, this time in a hay-rick *de luxe*, with straw and an old quilt on the slats of the floor. The Lettish officers examined me again, and told me that if I would take a hay-rick and drive twenty-two versts to the Kreisberg station I could take a train at two in the morning that would bring me to Riga early the next afternoon. They gave me food, produced a hay-rick, and, half frozen but safe, I reached Kreizberg and finally Riga, at one the next afternoon.

Feeling secure at last, I left the station at Riga and proceeded up the street towards the De Rome Hotel. I noticed an aeroplane circling overhead, but I had grown so accustomed to war manœuvers that I disregarded it entirely. About two squares further on my way I heard a terrific crash and explosion and turned to see smoke rising from the station I had just left. A German aeroplane had bombed the station, killing seven people and injuring fourteen.

Arrived at the hotel, I asked the proprietor what was wrong. He told me that the Germans were marching on the town, and shelling it as they marched, and that 60,000 of them were just across the river.

My only thought was that I wanted to get out at once. "You can't go," he said. "There are no boats running and the German army[3] controls the railroad to Mitau."

Apparently it was as dangerous to come out to civilization as it had been to go into "barbarous" Soviet Russia. I recalled the peace and the kindness I had found inside that supposedly violent land with a great longing.

That afternoon I went to the Lettish Foreign Office to visit the officials who had granted me permission to enter a few weeks before. They appeared glad to see me, but incredulous as to my identity. Was I sure that I had been safely through Russia? Was I still in the flesh or merely a very vigorous and somewhat pugnacious ghost? My young friend who had been so concerned was very eager to know

[3] This was the Army of Von der Glotz.

what I had seen. I told him I could indeed confirm his worst fears. The Bolsheviki were people who had but little respect for the sacred rights of private property. I hastened to make my escape before he could ask me about the nationalization of women. I did not want to disappoint him too much.

The next day all the guests of the hotel were locked in and forbidden to leave the hotel. The Lettish staff officers were established in the hotel, two doors away from my room. Two regiments of Esthonians reached Riga that day and their first act was to place a big field-gun immediately in front of the hotel and begin firing over the roof of it into the German position. Knowing the reputation of the Germans for finding gun positions, I was not very sanguine over the prospects of my safe return to America. The shelling lasted for forty-eight hours, during which time the deafening noise and the jarring of the walls made rest impossible.

The Danish Consul and his staff occupied the rooms immediately across the hall from mine. The third day they invited me over to lunch with them in their room, as Lettish soldiers had been billeted in the dining-room downstairs. About four in the afternoon, after the wine had all been consumed, the Danes began singing the songs of their own country. Scarcely an hour later the door of the room was opened and five Lettish officers marched in, ordering us all to "Get your clothes together and get ready." The Danish Consul asked what they meant. "You have been drinking the health of Germany and singing German songs. Yon are under arrest," was the answer.

I was somewhat disappointed when they apologized after we had shown them our papers. Arrest and deportation to other shores seemed very attractive to me just then.

A little later the proprietor came in and told us that food was getting scarce, that prices had doubled, and that we would have to pay in Czarist rubles, since the Lettish rubles (which he had been glad to take before) were no longer any good. After we had organized a vigorous protest he recanted and we had no further difficulty on that score.

The next day Michael Farbman of the *Chicago Tribune*, with G. G. Desmond of the *London Daily News*, dropped in from somewhere and told me there would be a chance that Sunday night of going to Copenhagen on a British destroyer. Since Desmond was a British subject we chose him to take up the matter with the British mission. His efforts were successful, and we left the hotel under cover of darkness and, hugging the walls of the buildings, we finally reached the British mission. In company with several English officers we started through the dark streets at seven-thirty in the evening with shells falling everywhere, and walked three miles to the bend of the Dvina, out of range of the firing. Twice we were shot at by Lettish outposts who had not been informed that we were supposed to pass. Luckily for us they proved to be bad shots, and the shouts of "English, English" from the officers stopped the firing. At nine in the evening we reached the river and were bundled into two small boats, pulled by a slow-going gasoline launch. The Letts were on one side of the river; the Germans on the other, and both sides impartially fired at us with their rifles, but although they hit each boat once they did not touch us. I shall never forget the English officers, crouching in the bottoms of the boats—beside me—shouting "English, English" at the top of their voices as we proceeded, and persisting in their shouting of the word that had hitherto proven a magic one, in spite of the fact that it could not possibly be heard by either side, and forgetting, apparently, that if it were heard by the Germans it might not deter them.

After two and one-half hours of this, during which we traversed eight miles, we reached the gulf and the comparative safety of the British cruiser *Abdiel.* At last my troubles were over.

We were to leave for Copenhagen the next morning. However, at ten the next morning we were transferred from the *Abdiel* to the *Princess Margaret,* a Canadian Royal steamer which had been converted into a mine-layer during the war, and had come into the harbor the night before, on her way to Riga with a cargo of goods. She could not proceed up the river because of the firing. English officers and all were transferred to this ship, because the *Abdiel* was not leaving and there was no telling when the *Princess Margaret* would leave. For three days we were kept on this boat. During this time more than a hundred refugees from Riga were added to its list. Eight or nine British cruisers and destroyers were lying at anchor in the Gulf, and on our second morning on the *Princess Margaret* we learned that the English had given the Germans until that time to evacuate their positions, after which they would open fire. The Germans had refused, and the bombarding began. The *Princess Margaret* stood out of range, but we could see with glasses the effects of the bombardment, which lasted the whole afternoon, until finally the German guns were silenced and the Letts crossed the river.

That evening we heard that the destroyer *Cleopatra* was sailing the next morning for Copenhagen and England and would come alongside to take mail, and that the English officers on the *Princess Margaret* were going on the *Cleopatra.* Farbman and I sent Desmond to the captain to get permission for us to go also, which he obtained after some persuasion. The others remained—and may be there still.

At eight the next morning the *Cleopatra* came toward us, but the sea was running high and she could not approach nearer than a hundred yards. A lifeboat was lowered from the *Princess,* our baggage thrown in, and we descended on rope ladders to the swaying and tossing boat below. I am a poor swimmer and the brief but exciting journey to the *Cleopatra* was occupied in meditation on my escape from shot and shell only to be drowned in the waters of the Gulf.

When we finally reached the *Cleopatra,* I was prepared for more delay, any amount of delay. I had grown so accustomed to it that I thought it would save my nerves from further strain to take it for granted. However we started almost immediately. This was Friday morning, October 17th. We reached Copenhagen Saturday, October 18th, at six in the evening. At last I had escaped the roar of cannon and the sound of bursting shells. The relief and the peace of Copenhagen could only be compared with the peace I had found in "Barbarous Soviet Russia."

APPENDIX

CODE OF LABOR LAWS

SOVIET RUSSIA'S CODE OF LABOR LAWS

I. The Code of Labor Laws shall take effect immediately upon its publication in the *Compilation of Laws and Regulations of the Workmen's and Peasants' Government.* This Code must be extensively circulated among the working class of the country by all the local organs of the Soviet Government and be posted in a conspicuous place in all Soviet Institutions.

II. The regulations of the Code of Labor Laws shall apply to all persons receiving remuneration for their work and shall be obligatory for all enterprises, institutions and establishments (Soviet, public, private and domestic), as well as for all private employers exploiting labor.

III. All existing regulations and those to be issued on questions of labor, of a general character (orders of individual establishments, instructions, rules of internal management, etc.), as well as individual contracts and agreements, shall be valid only in so far as they do not conflict with this Code.

IV. All labor agreements previously entered into, as well as all those which will be entered into in the future, in so far as they contradict the regulations of this Code, shall not be considered valid or obligatory, either for the employees or the employers.

V. In enterprises and establishments where the work is carried on in the form of organized cooperation (Section 6, Labor Division A of the present Code) the wage earners must be allowed the widest possible self-government under the supervision of the Central Soviet authorities. On this basis alone can the working masses be successfully educated in the spirit of socialist and communal government.

VI. The labor conditions in the communal enterprises organized as well as supported by the Soviet institutions (agricultural and other communes) are regulated by special rules of the All-Russian Central Executive Committee and of the Council of People's Commissars, and by instructions of the People's Commissariat of Agriculture and Labor.

The labor conditions of farmers on land assigned them for cultivation are regulated by the Code of Rural Laws.

The labor conditions of independent artisans are regulated by special rules of the Commissariat of Labor.

ARTICLE I
ON COMPULSORY LABOR

1. All citizens of the Russian Socialist Federated Soviet Republic, with the exceptions stated in Sections 2 and 3, shall be subject to compulsory labor.

2. The following persons shall be exempt from compulsory labor:

      (*a*) Persons under 16 years of age;

      (*b*) All persons over 50 years;

      (*c*) Persons who have become incapacitated by injury or illness.

3. Temporarily exempt from compulsory labor are:

      (*a*) Persons who are temporarily incapacitated owing to illness or injury, for a period necessary for their recovery.

      (*b*) Women, for a period of eight weeks before and eight weeks after confinement.

4. All students shall be subject to compulsory labor at the schools.

5. The fact of permanent or temporary disability shall be certified after a medical examination by the Bureau of Medical Survey in the city, district or province, by accident insurance office or agencies representing the former, according to the place of residence of the person whose disability is to be certified.

Note I. The rules on the method of examination of disabled workmen are appended hereto.

Note II. Persons who are subject to compulsory labor and are not engaged in useful public work may be summoned by the local Soviets for the execution of public work, on conditions determined by the Department of Labor in agreement with the local Soviets of trade unions.

6. Labor may be performed in the form of—

      (*a*) Organized cooperation;

      (*b*) Individual personal services;

      (*c*) Individual special jobs.

7. Labor conditions in government (Soviet) establishments shall be regulated by tariff rules approved by the Central Soviet authorities through the People's Commissariat of Labor.

8. Labor conditions in all establishments (Soviet, nationalized, public and private) shall be regulated by tariff rules drafted by the trade unions, in agreement with the directors or owners of establishments and enterprises, and approved by the People's Commissariat of Labor.

Note. In cases where it is impossible to arrive at an understanding with the directors or owners of establishments or enterprises, the tariff rules shall be drawn up by the trade unions and submitted for approval to the People's Commissariat of Labor.

9. Labor in the form of individual personal service or in the form of individual special jobs shall be regulated by tariff rules drafted by the respective trade unions and approved by the People's Commissariat of Labor.

ARTICLE II
THE RIGHT TO WORK

10. All citizens able to work have the right to employment at their vocations and for remuneration fixed for such class of work.

Note. The District Exchange Bureaus of the Department of Labor Distribution may, by agreement with the respective unions, assign individual wage earners or groups of them to work at other trades if there is no demand for labor at the vocations of the persons in question.

11. The right to work belongs first of all to those who are subject to compulsory labor.

12. Of the classes exempt from compulsory labor, only those mentioned in subdivision "*b*" of Section 2 have a right to work.

13. Those mentioned in subdivisions "*a*" and "*c*" of Section 2 are absolutely deprived of the right to work, and those mentioned in Section 3 temporarily deprived of the right to work.

14. All persons of the female sex, and those of the male sex under 18 years of age, shall have no right to work during night time or in those branches of industry where the conditions of labor are especially hard or dangerous.

Note. A list of especially hard and health-endangering occupations shall be prepared by the Department of Labor Protection of the People's Commissariat of Labor, and shall be published in the month of January of each year in the *Compilation of Laws and Regulations of the Workmen's and Peasants' Government.*

ARTICLE III
METHODS OF LABOR DISTRIBUTION

15. The enforcement of the right to work shall be secured through the Departments of Labor Distribution, trade unions, and through all the institutions of the Russian Socialist Federated Soviet Republic.

16. The assignment of wage earners to work shall be carried out through the Departments of Labor Distribution.

17. A wage earner may be summoned to work, save by the Departments of Labor Distribution, only when chosen for a position by a Soviet institution or enterprise.

18. Vacancies may be filled by election when the work offered requires politi-

cal reliability or unusual special knowledge, for which the person elected is noted.

19. Persons engaged for work by election must register in the Department of Labor Distribution before they are accepted, but they shall not be subject to the rules concerning probation set forth in Article IV of the present Code.

20. Unemployed persons shall be assigned to work through the Departments of Labor Distribution in the manner stated in Sections 21–30.

21. A wage earner who is not engaged on work at his vocation shall register in the local Department of Labor Distribution as unemployed.

22. Establishments and individuals in need of workers should apply to the Local Department of Labor Distribution or its division (Correspondence Bureau) stating the condition of the work offered as well as the requirements which the workmen must meet (trade, knowledge, experience).

23. The Department of Labor Distribution, on receipt of the application mentioned in Section 22, shall assign the persons meeting the requirements thereof in the order determined by the same.

24. An unemployed person has no right to refuse an offer of work at his vocation, provided the working conditions conform with the standards fixed by the respective tariff regulations, or in the absence of the same by the trade unions.

25. A wage worker engaged for work for a period of not more than two weeks, shall be considered unemployed, and shall not lose his place on the list of the Department of Labor Distribution.

26. Should the Local Department of Labor Distribution have no workers on its lists meeting the stated requirements, the application must be immediately sent to the District Exchange Bureau, and the establishment or individual offering the employment shall be simultaneously notified to this effect.

27. Whenever workers are required for work outside of their district, a roll-call of the unemployed registered in the Department of Labor Distribution shall take place, to ascertain who are willing to go; if a sufficient number of such should not be found, the Department of Labor Distribution shall assign the lacking number from among the unemployed in the order of their registration, provided that those who have dependents must not be given preference, before single persons.

28. If in the Departments of Labor Distribution, within the limits of the district, there be no workmen meeting the requirements, the District Exchange Bureau has the right, upon agreement with the respective trade union, to send unemployed of another class approaching as nearly as possible the trade required.

29. An unemployed person who is offered work outside his vocation shall be obliged to accept it, on the understanding, if he so wishes, that this be only temporary, until he receives work at his vocation.

30. A wage earner who is working outside his specialty, and who has stated his wish that this be only temporary, shall retain his place on the register on the Department of Labor Distribution until he gets work at his vocation.

31. Private individuals violating the rules of labor distribution set forth in this article shall be punished by the order of the local board of the Department of Labor Distribution by a fine of not less than 300 rubles or by arrest for not less than one week. Soviet establishments and officials violating these rules on labor distribution shall be liable to criminal prosecution.

ARTICLE IV
PROBATION PERIODS

32. Final acceptance of workers for permanent employment shall be preceded by a period of probation of not more than six days; in Soviet institutions the probation period shall be two weeks for unskilled and less responsible work and one month for skilled and responsible work.

33. According to the results of the probation the wage earner shall either be given a permanent appointment, or rejected with payment for the period of probation in accordance with the tariff rates.

34. The results of the probation (acceptance or rejection) shall be communicated to the Department of Labor Distribution.

35. Up to the expiration of the probation period, the wage earner shall be considered as unemployed, and shall retain his place on the eligible list of the Department of Labor Distribution.

36. A person who, after probation, has been rejected, may appeal against this decision to the union of which he is a member.

37. Should the trade union consider the appeal mentioned in the preceding section justified, it shall enter into negotiations with the establishment or person who has rejected the wage earner, with the request to accept the complainant.

38. In ease of failure of negotiations mentioned in Section 37, the matter shall be submitted to the Local Department of Labor, whose decision shall be final and subject to no further appeal.

39. The Department of Labor may demand that the person or establishment provide with work the wage earner who has been rejected without sufficient reason. Furthermore, it may demand that the said person or establishment compensate the wage earner according to the tariff rates for the time lost between his rejection and his acceptance pursuant to the decision of the Department of Labor.

ARTICLE V
TRANSFER AND DISCHARGE OF WAGE EARNERS

40. The transfer of wage earners in all enterprises, establishments, or institutions employing paid labor, can take place only if it is required in the interest of the business and by the decision of the proper organ of management.

Note. This rule does not apply to work with private individuals employing paid labor, if the work is of the subdivisions mentioned in "*b*" and "*c*" of Section 6.

41. The transfer of a wage earner to other work within the enterprise, establishment or institution where he is employed may be ordered by the managing organs of said enterprise, establishment or institution.

42. The transfer of a wage earner to another enterprise, establishment or institution situated in the same or in another locality, may be ordered by the corresponding organ of management with the consent of the Department of Labor Distribution.

43. The order of an organ of management to transfer a wage earner as mentioned in Section 40 may be appealed from to the respective Department of Labor (local or district) by the interested individuals or organizations.

44. The decision of the Department of Labor in the matter of the transfer of a wage earner may be appealed from by the interested parties to the District Department of Labor or to the People's Commissariat of Labor, whose decision in the matter in dispute is final and not subject to further appeal.

45. In case of urgent public work the District Department of Labor may, in agreement with the respective professional unions and with the approval of the People's Commissariat of Labor, order the transfer of a whole group of wage earners from the organization where they are employed to another situated in the same or in another locality, provided a sufficient number of volunteers for such work cannot be found.

46. The discharge of wage earners from an enterprise, establishment or institution where they have been employed is permissible in the following cases:

> (*a*) In case of complete or partial liquidation of the enterprise, establishment or institution, or of cancellation of certain orders or work;

> (*b*) In case of suspension of work for more than a month;

> (*c*) In case of expiration of term of employment or of completion of the job, if the work was of a temporary character;

> (*d*) In case of evident unfitness for work, by special decision of the organs of management and subject to agreement with the respective professional unions.

> (*e*) By request of the wage earner.

47. The organ of management of the enterprise, establishment or institution where a wage earner is employed, or the person for whom a wage earner is working must give the wage earner two weeks' notice of the proposed discharge, for the reasons mentioned in "*a*," "*b*" and "*d*" of Section 46, notifying simultaneously the Local Department of Labor Distribution.

48. A wage earner discharged for the reasons mentioned in subdivisions "*a*," "*b*" and "*d*" of Section 46 shall be considered unemployed and entered as such on the lists of the Department of Labor Distribution and shall continue to perform his work until the expiration of the term of two weeks mentioned in the preceding section.

49. The order to discharge an employee for the reasons mentioned in sub-divisions "*a*," "*b*" and "*d*" of Section 46 may be appealed from by the interested persons to the Local Department of Labor.

50. The decision of the Local Department of Labor on the question of discharge may be appealed from by either party to the District Department of Labor, whose decision on the question in dispute is final and not subject to further appeal.

51. Discharge by request of the wage earner from enterprise, establishment or institution must be preceded by an examination of the reasons for the resignation by the respective organ of workmen's self-government (works and other committees).

Note. This rule does not apply to the resignation of a wage earner employed by an individual, if the work is of the character mentioned in subdivisions "*b*" and "*c*" of Section 6.

52. If the organ of workers' self-government (works or other committee) after investigating the reasons for the resignation finds the resignation unjustified the wage earner must remain at work, but may appeal from the decision of the Committee to the respective professional union.

53. A wage earner who quits work contrary to the decision of the Committee, pursuant to Section 52, shall forfeit for one week the right to register with the Department of Labor Distribution.

54. Institutions and persons employing paid labor shall inform the Local Department of Labor Distribution and the respective professional union of each wage earner who quits work, stating the date and the reason thereof.

ARTICLE VI
REMUNERATION OF LABOR

55. The remuneration of wage earners for work in enterprises, establishments and institutions employing paid labor, and the detailed conditions and order of payment shall be fixed by tariffs worked out for each kind of labor in the manner described in Sections 7–9 of the present Code.

56. All institutions working out the tariff rates must comply with the provisions of this article of the Code of Labor Laws.

57. In working out the tariff rates and determining the standard remuneration rates, all the wage earners of a trade shall be divided into groups and categories and a definite standard of remuneration shall be fixed for each of them.

58. The standard of remuneration fixed by the tariff rates must be at least sufficient to cover the minimum living expenses as determined by the People's Commissariat of Labor for each district of the Russian Socialist Federated Soviet Republic and published in the *Compilation of Laws and Regulations of the Workmen's and Peasants' Government.*

59. In determining the standard of remuneration for each group and category attention shall be given to the kind of labor, the danger of the conditions, under

which the work is performed, the complexity and accuracy of the work, the degree of independence and responsibility as well as the standard of education and experience required for the performance of the work.

60. The remuneration of each wage earner shall be determined by his classification in a definite group and category.

61. The classification of wage earners into groups and categories within each branch of labor shall be done by special valuation commissions, local and central, established by the respective professional organizations.

Note. The procedure of the valuation commissions shall be determined by the People's Commissariat of Labor.

62. The tariff regulations shall fix the standard of remuneration for a normal working day or for piece-work, and particularly the remuneration for overtime work.

63. Remuneration for piece-work shall be computed by dividing the daily tariff rate by the number of pieces constituting the production standard.

64. The standard of remuneration fixed for overtime work shall not exceed time and a half of the normal remuneration.

65. Excepting the remuneration paid for overtime work done in the same or in a different branch of labor, no additional remuneration in excess of the standard fixed for a given group and category shall be permitted, irrespective of the pretext and form under which it might be offered and whether it be paid in only one or in several places of employment.

66. Persons working in several places must state in which place of employment they wish to receive their pay.

67. Persons receiving excessive remuneration, in violation of Section 65, shall be liable to criminal prosecution for fraud, and the remuneration received in excess of the normal (standard) may be deducted from subsequent payments.

68. From the remuneration of the wage earner may be deducted the excess remuneration received in violation of Section 65, and the remuneration earned by the wage earner during his vacation; deduction may also be made for cessation of work.

69. No other deductions, except those mentioned in Section 68, shall be permitted, irrespective of the form or pretext under which they might be made.

70. Payment of remuneration must not be made in advance.

71. If the work is steady, payment for the same must be made periodically, at least once in every fortnight. Remuneration for temporary work and for special jobs provided the same continues at least for two weeks, shall be paid immediately upon completion of work.

72. Payments shall be made in money or in kind (lodgings, food supplies, etc.)

73. To make payments in kind special permission must be obtained from the Local Department of Labor which shall determine the rates jointly with the respec-

tive trade unions.

Note. The rates thus determined must be based on the standard prices fixed by the respective institutions of the Soviet authority (valuation commissions of the Commissariat of Victuals, Land and Housing Department, Price Committee, etc.)

74. Payments must take place during working hours.

75. Payments must be made at the place of work.

76. The wage earner shall be paid only for actual work done. If a cessation of work is caused during the working day by circumstances beyond the control of the wage earner (through accident or through the fault of the administration), he shall be paid for the time lost on the basis of the daily tariff rates, if he does time work, or on the basis of his average daily earning, if he does piece-work.

77. A wage earner shall be paid his wage during leave of absence (Sections 106–107).

78. During illness of a wage earner the remuneration due him shall be paid as a subsidy from the hospital funds.

Note. The manner of payment of the subsidy is fixed by rules appended hereto.

79. Unemployed shall receive a subsidy out of the funds for unemployed.

Note. Rules concerning unemployed and the payment of subsidies to them are appended hereto.

80. Every wage earner must have a labor booklet in which all matters pertaining to the work done by him as well as the payments and subsidies received by him are entered.

Note. Rules regarding labor booklets for wage earners are appended hereto.

ARTICLE VII
WORKING HOURS

81. Working hours are regulated by the tariff rules made for each kind of labor, in the manner described in Sections 7–9 of the present Code.

82. The rules for working hours must conform with the provisions of this article of the Code of Labor Laws.

83. A normal working day shall mean the time fixed by the tariff regulations for the production of a certain amount of work.

84. The duration of a normal working day must in no case exceed eight hours for day work and seven hours for night work.

85. The duration of a normal day must not exceed six hours: (*a*) for persons under 18 years of age, and (*b*) in especially hard or health-endangering branches of industry (note Section 14 of the present Code).

86. During the normal working day time must be allowed for meals and for rest.

87. During recess machines, beltings and lathes must be stopped, unless this be impossible owing to technical conditions or in cases where these machines, beltings, etc., serve for ventilation, drainage, lighting, etc.

88. The time of recess fixed by Section 86 is not included in the working hours.

89. The recess must take place not later than four hours after the beginning of the working day, and must continue not less than a half hour and not more than two hours.

Note. Additional intermissions every three hours, and for not less than a half hour, must be allowed for working women nursing children.

90. The wage earners may use their free time at their own discretion. They shall be allowed during recess to leave the place of work.

91. In case the nature of the work is such that it requires a working day in excess of the normal, two or more shifts shall be engaged.

92. Where there are several shifts, each shift shall work the normal working hours; the change of shifts must take place during the time fixed by the rules of the internal management without interfering with the normal course of work.

93. As a general rule, work in excess of the normal hours (overtime work) shall not be permitted.

94. Overtime work may be permitted in the following exceptional cases:

(*a*) Where the work is necessary for the prevention of a public calamity or in case the existence of the Soviet Government of the R. S. F. S. R. or human life is endangered;

(*b*) An emergency, public work in relation to water supply, lighting, sewerage or transportation, in case of accident or extraordinary interruption of their regular operation;

(*c*) When it is necessary to complete work which, owing to unforeseen or accidental delay due to technical condition of production, could not be completed during the normal working hours. If leaving the work uncompleted would cause damage to materials or machinery;

(*d*) On repairs or renewal of machine parts or construction work, wherever necessary to prevent stoppage of work by a considerable number of wage earners.

95. In the case described in subdivision "*c*" of Section 94, overtime work is permissible only with the consent of the respective trade union.

96. For overtime work described in subdivision "*d*" of Section 94, permission must be obtained from the local labor inspector, in addition to the permit mentioned in the preceding section.

97. No females and no males under 18 years of age may do any overtime work.

98. The time spent on overtime work in the course of two consecutive days

must not exceed four hours.

99. No overtime work shall be permitted to make up for a wage earner's tardiness in reporting at his place of work.

100. All overtime work done by a wage earner, as well as the remuneration received by him for the same, must be recorded in his labor booklet.

101. The total number of days on which overtime may be permitted in any enterprise, establishment or institution must not exceed 50 days per annum, including such days when only one wage earner worked overtime.

102. Every enterprise, establishment or institution must keep a special record book for overtime work.

103. All wage earners must be allowed a weekly uninterrupted rest of not less than 42 hours.

104. No work shall be done on specially designated holidays.

Note. Rules concerning holidays and days of weekly rest are appended hereto.

105. On the eve of rest days the normal working day shall be reduced by two hours.

Note. This section shall not apply to institutions and enterprises where the working day does not exceed six hours.

106. Every wage earner who has worked without interruption not less than six months shall be entitled to leave of absence for two weeks, irrespective of whether he worked in only one or in several enterprises, establishments or institutions.

107. Every wage earner who has worked without interruption not less than a year shall be entitled to leave of absence for one month, irrespective of whether he worked in only one or in several enterprises, establishments or institutions.

Note. Sections 106 and 107 shall take effect beginning January 1, 1919.

108. Leave of absence may be granted during the whole year, provided that the same does not interfere with the normal course of work in enterprise, establishment or institution.

109. The time and order in which leave of absence may be granted shall be determined by agreement between the management of enterprise, establishment or institution and proper self-government bodies of the wage earners (works and other committees).

110. A wage earner shall not be allowed to work for remuneration during his leave of absence.

111. The remuneration of a wage earner earned during his leave of absence shall be deducted from his regular wages.

112. The absence of a wage earner from work caused by special circumstances and permitted by the manager shall not be counted as leave of absence; the wage earner shall not be paid for the working hours lost in such cases.

ARTICLE VIII
METHODS TO ASSURE EFFICIENCY OF LABOR

113. In order to assure efficiency of labor, every wage earner working in an enterprise, establishment or institution (governmental, public or private) employing labor in the form of organized collaboration, as well as the administration of the enterprise, establishment or institution, shall strictly observe the rules of this article of the Code relative to standards of efficiency, output and rules of internal management.

114. Every wage earner must during a normal working day and under normal working conditions perform the standard amount of work fixed for the category and group in which he is enrolled.

Note. Normal conditions referred to in this section, shall mean:

(*a*) Good condition of machines, lathes and accessories;

(*b*) Timely delivery of materials and tools necessary for the performance of the work;

(*c*) Good quality of materials and tools;

(*d*) Proper hygienic and sanitary equipment of the building where the work is performed (necessary lighting, heating, etc.).

115. The standard output for wage earners of each trade and of each group and category shall be fixed by valuation commissions of the respective trade unions (Section 62.)

116. In determining the standard output the valuation commission shall take into consideration the quantity of products usually turned out in the course of a normal working day and under normal technical conditions by the wage earners of the particular trade group and category.

117. The production standards of output adopted by the valuation commission must be approved by the proper Department of Labor jointly with the Council of National Economy.

118. A wage earner systematically producing less than the fixed standard may be transferred by decision of the proper valuation commission to other work in the same group and category, or to a lower group or category, with a corresponding reduction of wages.

Note. The wage earner may appeal from the decision to transfer him to a lower group or category with a reduction of wages, to the Local Department of Labor and from the decision of the latter to the District Department of Labor, whose decision shall be final and not subject to further appeal.

119. If a wage earner's failure to maintain the standard output be due to lack of good faith and to negligence on his part, he may be discharged in the manner set forth in subdivision "*d*" of Section 46 without the two weeks' notice prescribed by Section 47.

120. The Supreme Council of National Economy jointly with the People's

Commissariat of Labor may direct a general increase or decrease of the standards of efficiency and output for all wage earners and for all enterprises, establishments and institutions of a given district.

121. In addition to the regulations of the present article relative to standards of efficiency and output in enterprises, establishments and institutions, efficiency of labor shall be secured by rules of internal management.

122. The rules of internal management in Soviet institutions shall be made by the organs of Soviet authority with the approval of the People's Commissariat of Labor or its local departments.

123. The rules of internal management in industrial enterprises and establishments (Soviet, nationalized, private and public) shall be made by the trade unions and certified by the proper Departments of Labor.

124. The rules of internal management must include clear, precise and, as far as possible, exhaustive directions in relation to—

> (*a*) The general obligations of all wage earners (careful handling of all materials and tools, compliance with instructions of the managers regarding performance of work, observance of the fixed standard of working hours, etc.);

> (*b*) The special duties of the wage earners of the particular branch of industry (careful handling of the fire in enterprises using inflammable materials, observance of special cleanliness in enterprises producing food products, etc.);

> (*c*) The limits and manner of liability for breach of the above duties mentioned above in subdivisions "*a*" and "*b*."

125. The enforcement of the rules of internal management in Soviet institutions is entrusted to the responsible managers.

126. The enforcement of the rules of internal management in industrial enterprises and establishments (Soviet, nationalized, public or private) is entrusted to the self-government bodies of the wage earners (works or similar committees).

ARTICLE IX
PROTECTION OF LABOR

127. The protection of life, health and labor of persons engaged in any economic activity is entrusted to the labor inspection—the technical inspectors and the representatives of sanitary inspection.

128. The labor inspection is under the jurisdiction of the People's Commissariat of Labor and its local branches (Department of Labor) and is composed of elected labor inspectors.

129. Labor inspectors shall be elected by the Councils of Professional Unions.

Note I. The manner of election of labor inspectors shall be determined by the People's Commissariat of Labor.

Note II. In districts where there is no Council of Trade Unions, the Local Department of Labor shall summon a conference of representatives of the trade unions which shall elect the labor inspectors.

130. In performing the duties imposed upon them concerning the protection of the lives and health of wage earners the officers of labor inspection shall enforce the regulations of the present Code, and decrees, instructions, orders and other acts of the Soviet power intended to safeguard the lives and health of the workers.

131. For the attainment of the purposes stated in Section 130 the officers of labor inspection are authorized—

(*a*) To visit at any time of the day or night all the industrial enterprises of their districts and all places where work is carried on, as well as the buildings provided for the workmen by the enterprise (rooming houses, hospitals, asylums, baths, etc.);

(*b*) To demand of the managers of enterprises or establishments, as well as of the elective organs of the wage earners (works and similar committees) of those enterprises or establishments in the management of which they are participating, to produce all necessary books, records and information;

(*c*) To draw to the work of inspection representatives of the elective organizations of employees, as well as officials of the administration (managers, superintendents, foremen, etc.);

(*d*) To bring before the criminal court all violators of the regulations of the present Code, or of the decrees, instructions, orders and other acts of the Soviet authority intended to safeguard the lives and health of the wage earners;

(*e*) To assist the trade unions and works committees in their efforts to ameliorate the labor condition in individual enterprises as well as in whole branches of industry.

132. The officers of labor inspection are authorized to adopt special measures, in addition to the measures mentioned in the preceding section, for the removal of conditions endangering the lives and health of workmen, even if such measures have not been provided for by any particular law or regulation, instructions or order of the People's Commissariat of Labor or of the Local Department of Labor.

Note. Upon taking special measures to safeguard the lives and health of wage earners, as authorized by the present section, the officers of inspection shall immediately report to the Local Department of Labor, which may either approve these measures or reject them.

133. The scope and the forms of activity of the organs of labor inspection shall be determined by instructions and orders issued by the People's Commissariat of Labor.

134. The enforcement of the instructions, rules and regulations relating to safety is entrusted to the technical inspectors.

135. The technical inspectors shall be appointed by the Local Departments of Labor from among engineering specialists; these inspectors shall perform within the territory under their jurisdiction the duties prescribed by Section 31 of the present Code.

136. The technical inspectors shall be guided in their activity, besides the general regulations, by the instructions and orders of the People's Commissariat of Labor and by the instructions issued by the technical division of the Local Department of Labor.

137. The activity of the sanitary inspection shall be determined by instructions issued by the People's Commissariat of Health Protection in conference with the People's Commissariat of Labor.

APPENDIX TO SECTION 79
RULES CONCERNING UNEMPLOYED AND PAYMENT OF SUBSIDIES

1. An "unemployed" shall mean every citizen of the Russian Socialist Federated Soviet Republic subject to labor duty who is registered with the Local Department of Labor Distribution as being out of work at his vocation or at the remuneration fixed by the proper tariff.

2. An "unemployed" shall likewise mean:

   (*a*) Any person who has obtained employment for a term not exceeding two weeks (Section 25 of the present Code);

   (*b*) Any person who is temporarily employed outside his vocation, until he shall obtain work at his vocation (Sections 29 and 30 of the present Code).

3. The rights of unemployed shall not be extended—

   (*a*) To persons who in violation of Sections 2, 24 and 29 of the present Code, have evaded the labor duty, and refused work offered to them;

   (*b*) To persons not registered as unemployed with the Local Department of Labor Distribution (Section 21 of the present Code);

   (*c*) To persons who have wilfully quit work, for the term specified in Section 54 of the present Code.

4. All persons described in Section 1 and subdivision "*b*" of Section 2 of these rules shall be entitled to permanent employment (for a term exceeding two weeks) at their vocations in the order of priority determined by the list of the Department of Labor Distribution for each vocation.

5. Persons described in Section 1 and subdivision "*b*" of Article 2 of these rules shall be entitled to a subsidy from the local fund for unemployed.

6. The subsidy to unemployed provided in Section 1 of the present rules shall

be equal to the remuneration fixed by the tariff for the group and category on which the wage earner was assigned by the valuation commission (Section 61.)

Note. In exceptional cases the People's Commissariat of Labor may reduce the unemployed subsidy to the minimum of living expenses as determined for the district in question.

7. A wage earner employed temporarily outside of his vocation (Subdivision "*b*" of Section 2) shall receive a subsidy equal to the differences between the remuneration fixed for the group and category in which he is enrolled and his actual remuneration, in case the latter be less than the former.

8. An unemployed who desires to avail himself of his right to a subsidy shall apply to the local funds for unemployed and shall present the following documents: (*a*) his registration card from the Local Department of Labor Distribution; and (*b*) a certificate of the valuation commission showing his assignment to a definite group and category of wage earners.

9. Before paying the subsidy the local funds for unemployed shall ascertain, through the Department of Labor Distribution and the respective trade union, the extent of applicant's unemployment and the causes thereof, as well as the group and category to which he belongs.

10. The local funds for unemployed may for good reasons, be denied the applicant.

11. If an application is denied, the local fund for unemployed shall inform the applicant thereof within three days.

12. The decision of the local fund for unemployed may within two weeks, be appealed from by the interested parties to the Local Department of Labor, and the decision of the latter may be appealed from to the District Department of Labor. The decision of the District Department of Labor is final and subject to no further appeal.

13. The payment of the subsidy to an unemployed shall commence only after he has actually been laid off and not later than by the fifth day.

14. The subsidies shall be paid from: the fund of insurance for the unemployed.

15. The fund of unemployment insurance shall be made up,

    (*a*) from obligatory payments by all enterprises, establishments and institutions employing paid labor;

    (*b*) from fines imposed for default in such payments;

    (*c*) from casual payments.

16. The amount and the manner of collection of the payments and fines mentioned in Section 15 of these rules shall be determined every year by a special order of the People's Commissariat of Labor.

APPENDIX TO SECTION 80
RULES CONCERNING LABOR BOOKLETS

1. Every citizen of the Russian Socialist Federated Soviet Republic, upon assignment to a definite group and category (Section 62 of the present Code), shall receive, free of charge, a labor booklet.

Note. The form of the labor booklets shall be worked out by the People's Commissariat of Labor.

2. Each wage earner, on entering the employment of an enterprise, establishment or institution employing paid labor, shall present his labor booklet to the management thereof, or on entering the employment of a private individual—to the latter.

Note. A copy of the labor booklet shall be kept by the management of the enterprise, establishment, institution or private individual by whom the wage earner is employed.

3. All work performed by a wage earner during the normal working day as well as piece-work or overtime work, and all payments received by him as a wage earner (remuneration in money or in kind, subsidies from the unemployment and hospital funds), must be entered in his labor booklet.

Note. In the labor booklet must also be entered the leaves of absence and sick leave of the wage earner, as well as the fines imposed on him during and on account of his work.

4. Each entry in the labor booklet must be dated and signed by the person making the entry, and also by the wage earner (if the latter is literate), who thereby certifies the correctness of the entry.

5. The labor booklet shall contain:

(*a*) The name, surname and date of birth of the wage earner;

(*b*) The name and address of the trade union of which the wage earner is a member;

(*c*) The group and category to which the wage earner has been assigned by the valuation commission.

6. Upon the discharge of a wage earner, his labor booklet shall under no circumstances be withheld from him. Whenever an old booklet is replaced by a new one, the former shall be left in possession of the wage earner.

7. In case a wage earner loses his labor booklet, he shall be provided with a new one into which shall be copied all the entries of the lost booklet; in such a case a fee determined by the rules of internal management may be charged to the wage earner for the new booklet.

8. A wage earner must present his labor booklet upon the request:

(*a*) Of the managers of the enterprise, establishment or institution where he is employed;

(*b*) Of the Department of Labor Distribution;

(*c*) Of the trade union;

(*d*) Of the officials of workmen's control and of labor protection;

(*e*) Of the insurance offices or institutions acting as such.

APPENDIX TO SECTION 5
RULES FOR THE DETERMINATION OF DISABILITY FOR WORK

1. Disability for work shall be determined by an examination of the applicant by the Bureau of Medical Experts, in urban districts, or by the provincial insurance offices, accident insurance offices or institutions acting as such.

Note. In case it be impossible to organize a Bureau of Medical Experts at any insurance office, such a bureau may be organized at the Medical Sanitary Department of the local Soviet, provided, however, that the said bureau shall be guided in its actions by the general rules and instructions for insurance offices.

2. The staff of the Bureau of Experts shall include:

(*a*) Not less than three specialists in surgery;

(*b*) Representatives of the Board of Directors of the office;

(*c*) Sanitary mechanical engineers appointed by the Board of the office;

(*d*) Representatives of the trade unions.

Note. The specialists in surgery on the staff of the bureau shall be recommended by the medical sanitary department, with the consent of the Board of Directors, preferably from among the surgeons connected with the hospital funds, and shall be confirmed by a delegates' meeting of the office.

3. During the examination of a person at the Bureau of the Medical Commission, all persons who have applied for the examination may be present.

4. An application for the determination of the loss of working ability may be made by any person or institution.

5. Applications for examination shall be made to the insurance office nearest to the residence of the person in question.

6. Examinations shall take place in a special room of the insurance office.

Note. If the person to be examined cannot be brought to the insurance office, owing to his condition, the examination may take place at his residence.

7. Every person who is to be examined at the Bureau of Medical Experts shall be informed by the respective insurance office of the day and hour set for the examination and of the location of the section of the Bureau of Medical Experts where the same is to take place.

8. The Bureau of Medical Experts may use all methods approved by medical science for determining disability for work.

9. The Bureau of Medical Experts shall keep detailed minutes of the confer-

ence meetings, and the record embodying the results of the examinations shall be signed by all members of the bureau.

10. A person who has undergone an examination and has been found unfit for work shall receive a certificate from the Bureau of Medical Experts.

Note. A copy of the certificate shall be kept in the files of the bureau.

11. The records as well as the certificates shall show whether the disability is of a permanent or temporary character. If the disability for work be temporary, the record and certificate shall show the date set for examination.

12. After the disability for work has been certified the proper insurance office shall inform thereof the Department of Social Security of the local Soviet, stating the name, surname and address of the person disabled, as well as the character of the disability (whether temporary or permanent).

13. The decision of the Bureau of Medical Experts certifying or denying the disability of the applicant may be appealed from by the interested parties to the People's Commissariat of Health Protection.

14. The People's Commissariat of Health Protection may either dismiss the appeal or issue an order for the re-examination of appellant by a new staff of the Bureau of Experts.

15. The decision of the new staff of the Bureau of Experts shall be final and subject to no further appeal.

16. Re-examinations to establish the recovery of working ability shall be conducted in the same manner as the first examination, with the observance of the regulations of the present article of the Code.

17. The expenses incurred in connection with the examination of an insured person shall be charged to the respective insurance office. The expenses incurred in connection with the examination of a person not insured shall be charged to the respective enterprise, establishment or institution.

18. The People's Commissariat of Labor may, if necessary, modify or amend the present rules for the determination of disability for work.

Rules concerning payment of sick benefits (subsidies) to wage earners:

1. Every wage earner shall receive in case of sickness a subsidy and medical aid from the local hospital fund of which he is a member.

Note I. Each person may be a member of only one insurance fund at a time.

Note II. A person who has been ill outside the district of the local hospital fund of which he is a member shall receive the subsidy from the hospital fund of the district in which he has been taken ill. All expenses thus incurred shall be charged to the hospital fund of which the particular person is a member.

2. The sick benefits shall be paid to a member of a hospital fund from the first day of his sickness until the day of his recovery, with the exception of those days during which he has worked and accordingly received remuneration from the enterprise, establishment or institution where he is employed.

3. The sick benefit shall be equal to the remuneration fixed for a wage earner of the respective group and category.

Note I. The group and category in which the wage earner is enrolled shall be ascertained by the local hospital fund through the Department of Labor Distribution or through the trade unions.

Note II. The subsidy for pregnant women and those lying-in shall be fixed by special regulations of the People's Commissariat of Labor.

Note III. In exceptional cases the People's Commissariat of Labor may reduce the subsidy to the minimum of living expenses as determined for the respective district.

4. Besides the subsidies, the hospital funds shall also provide for their members free medical aid of every kind (first aid, ambulatory treatment, home treatment, treatment in sanatoria or resorts, etc.)

Note. To secure medical aid any hospital fund may, independently or in conjunction with other local funds, organize and maintain its own ambulatories, hospitals, etc., as well as enter into agreements with individual physicians and establishments.

5. The resources of the local hospital funds shall be derived:

    (*a*) From obligatory payments by enterprises, establishments and institutions (Soviet, public and private) employing paid labor;

    (*b*) From fines for delay of payments;

    (*c*) From profits on the investments of the funds;

    (*d*) From casual payments.

Note. The resources of the local hospital funds shall be consolidated into one common fund of insurance against sickness.

6. The amount of the payments to local hospital funds by enterprises, establishments and institutions employing paid labor shall be periodically fixed by the People's Commissariat of Labor.

Note I. In case these obligatory payments be not paid within the time fixed by the local hospital funds, they shall be collected by the Local Department of Labor; moreover, in addition to the sum due, a fine of 10 per cent thereof shall be imposed for the benefit of the hospital fund.

Note II. In case the delay be due to the fault of the responsible managers of the particular enterprise, establishment, or institution, the fine shall be collected from the personal means of the latter.

7. The decision of the hospital funds may be appealed from within two weeks to the Department of Labor. The decision of the Department of Labor shall be final and subject to no further appeal.

8. The People's Commissariat of Labor may, whenever necessary, change or

amend the foregoing rules concerning sick benefits to wage earners.

THE SECOND ALL-RUSSIAN CONGRESS OF TRADES UNIONS (VOCATIONAL UNIONS)

RESOLUTIONS ADOPTED AT THE CONFERENCE
MOSCOW, JUNE 16TH TO 25TH, 1919

A year's work of the professional trades unions of Russia was completed by a new conference, the second one in its history—which shows how young our professional movement is as yet. The past year was unparalleled in the history of the entire international trade union movement, both according to the kind of activity as well as those circumstances under which our unions had to carry on their work.

It was a year of the dictatorship of the proletariat.

On the ruins of the demolished capitalist system, the proletariat of Russia has taken upon itself the task of building up a new, Socialist Russia. While struggling and conquering, it was gradually turning to constructive work—strengthening its dictatorship by taking possession of the entire apparatus of the country's economic administration.

The proletariat, organized into professional unions, constituted the vanguard of the Socialist revolution. The unions were the hotbeds of revolution, and it has fallen to their lot to solve the most complicated problems—in fact they took into their hands the management of all economic affairs, taking over the factories, the mills and the mines. This problem was difficult in itself, and its complexity was increased still further through the economic disintegration and chaos which were caused by the imperialist world war.

The Second All-Russian Conference of Trades Unions demonstrated that the Russian professional trades union movement has grown stronger during the year and that its organization has improved in both quantity and quality.

The qualitative progress made by the Russian trades union movement expressed itself in that marvelous intelligence which the Conference displayed in grappling with the complicated problems it had to face. If the first All-Russian Conference of Professional trades unions outlined a rough draft of a plan according to which the working class was to steer its course during the period of its supremacy, if at that first conference the delegates were groping in the dark, trying to feel the correct way,—the second Conference found the path sufficiently cleared to proceed forward toward the solution of new problems put forth by the life and practice of the professional movement. If at the First Conference we could only speak of regulating industry and controlling it, now, at this Second Conference, we can already tabulate the results of organization in the realm of industry by the efforts of the working class itself.

A big stride forward was made by the proletariat organized within professional trades unions, when in discussing the question of organization it pointed out clearly and definitely the place which the proletariat of the entire world is occupying under the present circumstances. The Conference has not only firmly and decisively drawn the line between its position and that of neutrality, but it took a definite stand in favor of recognizing "the revolutionary class struggle for the realization of Socialism through the dictatorship of the proletariat."

The quantitative growth of the Russian trades unions since the first Conference, notwithstanding the fact that the counter-revolution has snatched away a number of provinces (Siberia, Finland, the Donetz region, Caucasia, etc.), has resulted in a membership of 3,422,000 whereas only 2,500,000 members were represented at the First Conference. Thus, within one year the membership increased by almost one million. According to the All-Russian industrial groupings, the number of union members represented at the conference was distributed as follows:

Metal trades	400,000
Tanners	225,000
Members of Trade-Industrial Union (probably sales clerks)	200,000
Workers engaged in the food industry	140,000
Tailors	150,000
Chemists	80,000
Architectural and building trades	120,000
Wood-working trades	70,000
Printers	60,000
Railroad workers	450,000
Glass and chinaware workers	24,000
Water transportation workers	200,000
Postal-telegraphic employees	100,000
Sugar industry	100,000
Textile workers (according to data furnished by the local union)	711,000
Firemen	50,000
Oil miners and refiners	30,000
Chauffeurs	98,000
Bank employees	70,000
Domestic help	50,000
Waiters (in taverns)	50,000
Cigar and cigarette makers	30,000
Drug clerks	14,000
Foresters	5,000

According to the data furnished by the committee on credentials, there were 748 delegates at the Conference with the right to vote, and 131 with a voice. The political composition of the Conference (according to the results of an informal inquiry) was as follows: 374 Communists, 75 sympathizers, 15 Left Socialists-Revolutionists, 5 Anarchists, 18 Internationalists, 4 representatives of the Bund, 29 United Social-Democrats, 23 non-partisans, and 236 delegates did not state their party affiliations. The party registration bureaus showed entirely different results, which have been confirmed by the vote cast for the main resolutions. Thus, at the Communist bureau 600 persons have registered (this includes party members having the right to vote, sympathizers, and people with a voice only, but no vote), the Internationalists had 50 persons, and the United Social-Democrats had 70.

Geographically the delegates were represented as follows:

From Unions	Second Conference		First Conference	
The Northern Region	100	delegates	69	delegates
The Central Region	320	"	112	"
The Volga Region	144	"	25	"
The Ural Region	2	"	13	"
The Southern Region	31	"	62	"
The Western Region	30	"	..	"

From Soviets and Northern		
Region	29	"
Central Region	70	"
Ural Region	3	"
Southern Region	6	"
Western Region	14	"
Volga Region	30	"

The local Soviets of the Professional Unions were represented according to regions, as follows:

Central Region	36 cities	1,004,500 persons
Northern Region	16 cities	396,000 persons
Volga Region	19 cities	499,300 persons
Western Region	7 cities	73,800 persons
Southern Region	4 cities	64,000 persons
	————	—————
Total	82 cities	2,037,600 persons

At the preceding Conference	49 cities	1,888,353 persons

From June 16th to 25th, 1919, during the nine days of its work, the second All-Russian Congress of Trades Unions solved the fundamental questions of the Russian professional (trades union) movement. The Conference more precisely defined the place of the professional trades unions in a proletarian state, it has more concretely outlined the interrelations of the trades unions with the organs of administration and, above all, with the People's Commissariat of Labor. All other questions, such as the regulation of working hours and wages, the safeguarding of labor and the social insurance of laborers, the organization of production, and workmen's control have been solved on the basis of the experience of the past year.

The Russian professional unions entered upon a new era of proletarian activity. And the unions are already facing practical problems—to put into practice the principles and resolutions adopted and in all phases of its work to follow one direction, that of still further strengthening its power, and participating more closely in establishing the might of proletarian Russia.

THE PROBLEMS OF THE PROFESSIONAL TRADES UNIONS

(A resolution introduced by M. Tomsky)

One year of political and economic dictatorship of the proletariat and the growth of the workers' revolution the world over, have fully borne out the correctness of the position taken by the first All-Russian Conference of the Professional Trades Unions, who have unconditionally bound up the fate of the economically organized proletariat with that of the Workers' and Peasants' Government.

The attempt, under the flag of "unity" and "independence" of the trades union movement, to pit the economically organized proletariat against the organs of the political dictatorship of its own class, has led the groups which were supporting this slogan, to an open struggle against the Soviet Government and has placed them outside the ranks of the working class.

In the course of the practical cooperation with the Soviet Government in the work for the strengthening and organization of the nation's economic life, the professional trades unions have passed from control over industry to organization of industry, taking an active part in the management of individual enterprises as well as in the entire economic life of the country.

But the task of nationalization of all the means of production and the organization of society on the new principles of Socialism demands persistent and careful labor involving the reconstruction of the entire governmental apparatus, the creation of new organs of control, and regulation of production and distribution, based on the organization and activity of the laboring masses who are themselves directly interested in the results.

This makes it imperative for the trades unions to take a more active and energetic part in the work of the Soviet Government (through direct participation in all governmental institutions, through the organization of proletarian mass control over their actions, and the carrying out, by means of their organization, of individual problems with which the Soviet Government is confronted), to aid in the reconstruction of various governmental institutions and in the gradual replacement of the same by their own organizations by amalgamating the unions with the governmental institutions.

However, it would be a mistake at the given stage of development of the professional trades union movement with the insufficiently developed organization to convert immediately the unions into governmental organs and to amalgamate the two organizations as well as for the unions to usurp of their own accord the functions of governmental institutions.

The entire process of complete amalgamation of the professional unions with the organs of government administration must come as an absolutely inevitable result of their work, in complete and close cooperation and harmony and the preparation of the laboring masses, for the task of managing the governmental apparatus and all the institutions for the regulation of the country's economic life.

This, in its turn, places before the unions the problem of welding together the as yet unorganized proletarian and semi-proletarian masses into strong productive unions, initiating them, under the control of the proletarian unions, into the task of social reconstruction and the general work of strengthening their organizations, as regards centralization and smoothly working unions as well as the strengthening of professional discipline.

Directly participating in all fields of Soviet work, forming and supplying the man-power for the governmental institutions, the professional unions must, through this work for which they must enlist their own organizations as well as the laboring masses, educate and prepare them for the task of managing not only production but the entire apparatus of government.

PROFESSIONAL UNIONS AND THE COMMISSARIAT OF LABOR

(A resolution embodied in V. Schmidt's report)

Professional trades unions organized according to the scale of production, called upon to regulate the conditions of labor and production in the interests of the working class as a whole, under the conditions of proletarian dictatorship, are becoming gradually converted into economic associations of the proletariat, acquiring a nation-wide significance. On the other hand, the Commissariat of Labor, as an organ of the Workers' and Peasants' Government, in which the organized industrial proletariat is at the present moment playing a leading part, serves as an instrument for the introduction of the economic policy of the working class, utilizing for this purpose its apparatus and all the power vested in governmental authorities to enforce its laws and regulations.

Therefore, with a view to eliminating the duality in the united economic policy of the working class, it is necessary to recognize that all fundamental decisions of the supreme union organ—the Congress of Professional Unions—are to be adopted by the People's Commissariat of Labor and embodied in its proposed legislation and all special obligatory regulations bearing on the conditions of labor and production, must first be approved by a majority of the All-Russian Central Council of Professional Trades Unions.

The Conference fully approves of coordination and cooperation between the All-Russian Central Council of Trades Unions and the People's Commissariat of

Labor and suggests that the local councils (Soviets) of trades unions participate in the work of local branches (departments) of the Commissariat of Labor, on the basis of the relations prevailing between the central bodies, for which purpose the local councils of trades unions are to send their representatives into the leading Soviets and make up out of the union apparatus its subdivisions (tariff, social insurance, labor safeguarding, etc.)

In order to finally eliminate all duplication in the solution of questions concerning the conditions and regulation of labor by separate departments, the Conference suggests that the All-Russian Central Executive Committee and the Soviet of People's Commissaries concentrate all its efforts to the working out of standards regulating the conditions of work, wages, organization of labor, order of employing and discharging help, safeguarding labor, and social insurance, through the People's Commissariat of Labor.

THE PARTICIPATION OF THE UNIONS IN THE ORGANIZATION OF INDUSTRY

(A resolution on the report made by Comrade Rudzutak)

1. The process of taking over the control of the industries which is now being completed by the workers' government, places the vocational associations in a position where they are coming to play an ever more and more important part in the special fields of their activity.

2. Standing in close relationship to the actual production and thus being the natural guardians of industry against the remnants of the bureaucratic apparatus permeated by the traditions of the old regime, the unions must build a new Socialist order, in accordance with the fixed program of production based on a national plan for the utilization of the proper products and material.

3. In the interests of preserving a single plan of organization of production, management and distribution, it will be necessary to concentrate in one center all the units of production, which are now in the charge of various departments (Chief Artillery Department, Navy and War Departments, etc.)

4. The participation of the unions in the industrial management should consist in the working out of a system of activity for the regulating and managing organs as a whole, insofar as there is a possibility of some part or other of their membership not being permeated by the spirit of Socialistic constructive activity. The management of the leading departments and centers must be composed mainly of the representatives of professional unions, following an understanding between the corresponding All-Russian Industrial Association or the All-Russian Council of Trades Unions and the presiding officers of the Supreme Council of National Economy.

5. All delegates representing the trades unions within the administrative and regulating bodies are responsible to the corresponding unions and are to report on their activities at regular intervals.

6. In order to keep up the organic connection between the unions and the man-

agement of the government owned mills, the unions are to call conferences of the management of the largest enterprises, not less than once in two months, for the purpose of discussing and passing upon the most important practical questions arising in the process of work.

7. In order to convert the regulating and managing organs into a proletarian apparatus for constructive Socialist work and in order to obtain the cooperation in this work of the large masses of the more advanced workers, it is necessary to saturate all the organs of regulation and management with proletarian elements by means of placing in their ranks responsible workers who assert themselves within the central and local trade union groups.

8. Together with the part which the unions are playing in the matter of directing the industrial life along the channels fixed by the programs of production, based upon the subjugation of private interest to those of society as a whole, comes their activity in connection with the basic element of production—labor. Therefore, the decisions of the central trade union associations are obligatory insofar as they bear on the questions of wage scales, inspection of labor, internal regulations within the factories, standards of production and labor discipline.

9. Being placed in the position of organizers of production at a moment when Russia is now more than at any other time, affected by a shortage of various kinds of material which causes a reduction of the output, the unions must safeguard the proletariat against the possibility of its exhaustion or degeneration, as a class of producers, at this critical period, and to safeguard its nucleus against social disintegration and its absorption by other classes; it is therefore necessary:

> (*a*) wherever a shortage of raw material exists to reduce the working day or the number of days per week, keeping employed at the factory the largest possible number of workers.

> (*b*) to introduce, wherever the number of hours or days per week is reduced, obligatory attendance at technical and educational courses, so as to utilize the crisis for the purpose of lifting the technical and cultural level of the laboring masses.

10. At the same time, in view of the primary significance of actually supplying the mills with the necessary products, and the impossibility of increasing the productivity of labor and introducing discipline, unless this question is solved in a satisfactory manner, it is necessary to enable the trades unions to participate as closely as possible in the work of production and distribution of provisions.

WORKERS' CONTROL

(Resolution in connection with N. Glebov's report)

The Second All-Russian Congress of Vocational Unions, having heard the report on workers' control, recognizes the following:

1. Workers' control, which was the strongest revolutionary weapon in the hands of the labor organizations in their struggle against economic disruption and the sabotage practised by the employers in their struggle against the proletariat

for economic supremacy, has led the working class into direct participation in the organization of production.

2. The economic dictatorship of the working class has created new conditions which stirred up the activity of the large masses of the workers. Through their vocational associations the workers have been called upon to organize the country's economic life and to participate in the management of production.

3. At the same time the working class domination over the economic life of the country has not as yet been completed. A subdued struggle is still seething within the new forms of economic life, which calls forth the necessity on the part of the laboring masses to control the activities of the institutions in charge of the management of production.

4. Under such conditions of transition from the capitalist system to the Socialist regime, the workers' control must develop, from a revolutionary weapon for the economic dictatorship of the proletariat, into a practical institution aiding in the strengthening of this dictatorship in the process of production.

5. The problems of workers' control must be confined to the supervision of the course of work in the various establishments, and to practically check on the activity of the management of individual mills as well as that of entire branches of industry. The workers' control is carried out in practice in a certain order according to which control does not precede, but, on the contrary, follows the executive work.

6. Workers' control is also to solve the problem of the gradual preparation of the large masses of the working class for direct participation in the matter of management and organization of industry.

With this object in view the Congress resolves:

1. To confirm the decision of the first All-Russian Congress of Vocational Unions regarding the formation of organs of control, both local and central, under the guidance of the vocational associations of the working class.

2. Within every nationalized industrial, commercial, and transport house, the local committee for control takes upon itself the supervision of the work of the enterprise and the activities of its management, for which purpose it gathers and systematizes all data relative to the running of the establishment and places the same at the disposal of the control department of their trade union, before which, whenever the necessity arises, the question of auditing the books of the enterprise is brought up.

> *Note.* In extraordinary cases the local control commission has the right on its own responsibility to fix the time for a revision of their enterprise, with a precise statement of the subject of control, on condition that the local control committee immediately notify to that effect the Department of Control of the corresponding industrial (vocational) union.

3. The local control committee is being formed of: (*a*) representatives of the corresponding industrial (vocational) union; (*b*) of the persons elected by the gen-

eral meeting of the workers employed in a given factory, who are subject to approval by the committee of the corresponding industrial (vocational) union. The members of the local control committee elected from among the committee of the industrial union, retain their office for a considerable length of time; while the persons elected at the general meeting are to be replaced in as short a period as possible, with a view to training the large masses of the people in the work of management and organization of industry so as to insure the gradual transition to the system of universal participation in it of all the workers.

4. The local control committee is responsible for its activities both before the general meeting of the workers of their factory and before the control department of their industrial (vocational) union. In case of abuse of authority, negligence in carrying out its duties, and so on, the local control committee is subject to severe punishment.

5. The representatives of the local control committee participate at the sessions of the management of the mill or factory, having only a voice, but no vote in the matter. The rights of administration of the establishment remains with the management and therefore the entire responsibility for the work of the enterprise rests with the management.

6. The coordination of the workers' control within the limits of any given industry must be centered within the industrial (vocational) union. The union creates a Workers' Control Department which is responsible before the management of its union.

7. The Congress authorizes the All-Russian Central Council (Soviet) of Vocational Unions to direct the institutions of workers' control. For this purpose the All-Russian Central Council is to form a supreme organ of workers' control, composed of the representatives of the industrial (vocational) unions.

8. With a view to coordinating all activities and eliminating the duplication of functions in the work of control, the organs of the People's Commissariat of State Control must work in contact with the controlling organs of the industrial (vocational) unions.

9. The supreme organ of workers' control is to work out the instructions, fully determining the rights and duties of the lower organs of control and their organization. Until such time as these instructions are made public the organs of workers' control in the nationalized enterprises are to be guided by these rulings.

10. The regulations for the workers' control of nationalized enterprises must be decreed by the Council of People's Commissaries.

11. In the establishments which have not been nationalized workers' control is to be carried out in accordance with the decree of November 14, 1917.

WAGE AND WORK REGULATION

(Resolution introduced in connection with V. Schmidt's report)

Observing a great variety and lack of coordination of the tariff (wage scale) regulations which hamper not only the standardization of labor, but their practical materialization, and explaining such an abnormal phenomenon in this matter by the presence of a number of glaring defects, (absence of a definite system of wages, which would serve as a basis of the tariff regulations, the elasticity of groups and categories, the elimination from these regulations of the salaries of the higher technical, commercial and administrative personnel), defects due to the rapid transition from one form of wage scale regulation to another; due to the weakness of the local unions and their local separatism, and, finally, the inconsistency (instability) of the local organs of governments in regard to the wage regulation policy, the Second All-Russian Congress of Vocational Unions deems it necessary to introduce the following amendments and additions to the wage regulations:

1. The basic principle of wage scale regulation, in connection with the struggle for the restoration of the country's economic forces, must be the responsibility of the laborers and other employees for the productivity of labor before their union, and the responsibility of the latter before the class associations of the proletariat. For this purpose the wage scale regulations must be based on the system of compensation of labor power which would serve as an incentive for the laborers to outdo each other in their desire to raise the productivity of labor in the nationalized enterprises, i.e. the piece-work and premium system founded on a rock-bottom standard of production, with a firmly fixed schedule of either increased pay or decreased hours of work in compensation for production above the standard requirements.

In those branches of industry where it is impossible to standardize the work, a scale of wages is to be applied on the basis of the time employed with definite hours of work and strict working regulations.

2. The wage scale of the industrial union is to include the higher technical, commercial and administrative personnel, whose salaries are to be subject to the control of the union. In accordance with this, the tariff regulation is to be divided into three fundamental parts; (*a*) the higher technical, commercial, and administrative personnel; (*b*) the lower technical and administrative personnel; the employees of the managements, the offices, institutions and commercial establishments, and (*c*) the laborers.

3. In order to eliminate too large a number of groups and categories (five groups and 15 categories) and to insure a fair compensation of the basic nucleus of the workers and other employees occupied in the industries, a subdivision into four groups and 12 categories is fixed for each of the three ranks (the higher personnel, the lower staff, the workers), the ratio of the higher wage to the lower within the limits of each one of the four given groups, from the first category to the 12th, is 1:1.75.

4. The wage scale regulations for individual groups of the workers and for certain branches of industry or parts thereof, must contain provisions either for the shortening of hours, or for the increase of pay as compensation for particularly harmful, dangerous, difficult or exhaustive labor, and in connection with climatic conditions.

5. Clothing and footwear is to be distributed to the workers engaged in the wood chopping industry, the sewerage and street cleaning industry, or occupied in underground work, work at a particularly high temperature, or necessitating the handling of harmful chemicals. Particularly difficult and harmful work (such as, underground work, the peat gathering industry, the preparation of wood fuel, work at a high temperature, work with poisonous gases and acids exhausting the system) should carry with it a home and a higher wage. This latter measure is to be carried out by the All-Russian and local councils of the Vocational Unions. In order to put these additions and amendments to the wage scale regulations into actual life and in order to do away with the obnoxious multiformity the Congress resolves:

To recognize the wage scale regulation which is being carried out on a national scale and which affects all the workers and employees of a given industry, from the highest administrator down to the skilled laborer,—as the one which best answers the fundamental needs of standardizing the wages.

To grant to the All-Russian Central Committee of the Industrial Unions the exclusive right to finally work out the wage scale regulations and to submit them for approval of the All-Russian Central Council of Professional Unions and to the People's Commissariat of Labor.

To deprive the local branches of the All-Russian centralized unions of the right to directly submit their wage scale for approval over the head of their central body, so long as an All-Russian industrial wage scale is in operation.

To leave to the local Soviets (councils) of the Vocational Unions the right to fix the wage scale regulations only for the local unions, which have no All-Russian association, using the wage scale regulations in force as a guide; under no circumstances changing the regulations passed on a national scale. Besides, it is the duty of the local Soviets of the Vocational Unions to coordinate individual scales in different industries while putting them into practice, and the right to present a grounded petition for the transfer of a given locality into another district in accordance with the proportional (percentage) scale of district decrease of wages.

The Congress approves of the work of the committee and the section on the construction of wage scale regulations and recommends to the All-Russian centralized industrial unions to accept them as a basis. The Congress authorizes the All-Russian Central Council of Vocational Unions to carry out this resolution strictly and without any deviations.

LABOR SAFEGUARDS AND SOCIAL INSURANCE OF THE WORKERS

(Resolution passed in connection with A. Bakhutov's report)

In capitalist society, with the complete economic and political supremacy of the bourgeoisie, the legal measures which were enacted for the safeguarding of labor and the individual kinds of social insurance of the workers were being enforced under the control of the capitalist state, together with the employing class, and beyond the reach of direct influence of the labor organizations. With the establishment of the dictatorship of the proletariat it became possible for the first time to put point blank all the questions arising out of the struggle against the grave consequences of the conditions of labor, which remain as a legacy of the capitalist era, as well as preventive measures and the solutions of the questions, in accordance with the Socialist aims of the present moment. The actual safeguarding of labor and the social insurance of the worker, with a view to safeguarding his life and increasing his strength and power, proved to be indissoluble aspects of the same problem—changing of conditions of labor, the reconstruction of the industrial environment in which the worker is laboring, and the betterment of his living conditions.

The October revolution determined the basic principles of social defence for the proletariat of Russia, having given over the safeguarding of labor and social insurance of the toilers into the hands of the working class, and for the first time it has created organs of factory inspection on the basis of elective representation.

But the acute civil war and the economic work of organization, as the fundamental problem which has been confronting the working class during the first year of the October *coup d'état*, have diverted the attention of the proletariat from a problem of no lesser significance—the safeguarding of its health, as the main source of national economy—and its economic organizations became indifferent. This is the reason why the working class paid but very little attention to questions of labor safeguards and social insurance, as well as to the institutions in charge of these questions.

At the present moment, however, the building of a new life, the reconstruction of the conditions of labor on a Socialist foundation, the safeguarding of production for the life and health of the workers, the betterment of their living conditions, the workers' insurance against all accidents depriving him of his labor power, the amalgamation of the various kinds of insurance agencies into one powerful organization, and the management of the same, are becoming the most important problems which the vocational unions are to solve. Together with the economic work of organization which includes the safeguarding of labor, social insurance of the toilers must take the proper place in the every-day work of the unions.

Taking all this into consideration, the second Congress of Vocational Unions finds it necessary that the vocational unions—

1. Take active part in the construction of united government insurance bodies through the formation of corresponding subdivisions within the departments of labor of the local Soviets, in accordance with the instructions of the Department of Social Insurance and Labor Safeguards of the People's Commissariat of Labor; 2. That they energetically carry out the "regulations of social insurance of the workers" of October 31st, 1918; 3. That they immediately start the organization within the unions of permanent committees on the safeguarding of labor, and of *nuclei* for the same within the various mills and factories for the purpose of cooperating with the governmental institutions charged with the safeguarding of labor; 4. That they intensify the work on the spot for the creation of labor inspection by

means of selection and training for this purpose of the active workers; 5. That they practically spread the validity of the safeguarding of labor regulations and their enforcement over all types of labor (in the building trades, in the transport service, over domestic servants, commercial and office workers, restaurant help, and agricultural workers); 6. That they pay particular attention to the conditions of labor in the small semi-handicraft establishments; 7. That they assist in the practical efforts of labor inspection to remove the children from the works and for the introduction of a shorter work-day for minors, enabling them at the same time to continue their education; 8. That they take an active part in the organization of local sanitary-hygienic and technical investigations of the conditions at the factories and mills, and in the working out of various obligatory standards and various measures for the safeguarding of labor; 9. That they carry out the principles of labor safeguarding through the current activity of the local and central organs regulating the nation's economy; 10. That they take an active part in the work of improving the living conditions of the working population; 11. That they energetically push the agitational and educational work among the proletarian masses along the lines of vocational hygiene and sanitation and the technique of insuring safety, as well as on general questions of social insurance and labor safeguarding.

THE INTERRELATION OF THE DEPARTMENT OF SOCIAL INSURANCE AND LABOR SAFEGUARDS OF THE PEOPLE' S COMMISSARIAT OF LABOR AND THE PEOPLE'S COMMISSARIAT OF SOCIAL INSURANCE

Whereas in the process of development of the social revolution the division of society into a handful of parasites, on the one hand, and into the masses of workers and peasants overloaded with excessive toil, on the other, is constantly disappearing, and the entire population is being transformed into a mass of producers who must be insured, in accordance with the provisions of the regulations on social insurance of the laborers, of October 31, 1918, against all accidents that might incapacitate them, and

Whereas the work of social insurance can be developed on condition of immediate participation of vocational unions through the medium of the corresponding organs of the People's Commissariat of Labor,

The second Congress of Vocational Unions holds that all insurance business, its functions, the institutions of the People's Commissariat of Social Insurance, affecting the workers, must be amalgamated into the common work of the Department of Social Insurance and Labor Safeguard of the People's Commissariat of Labor.

Having discussed the question of interrelations between the Commissariat of Public Health and the Department of Social Insurance and Labor Safeguards of the People's Commissariat of Labor, the second All-Russian Congress of Vocational Unions resolved to accept the following principles as a basis for the solution of the question:

1. Social insurance and labor safeguarding being a complete and logically unit-

ed institution, with the dictatorship of the proletariat in power, when the entire population of the Russian Socialist Federal Soviet Republic is being transformed into laborers, covers the activities of Commissariat of Health, thus representing under the circumstances one of the most important and most necessary links of one chain.

2. It is possible to carry into life the measures of social insurance and labor safeguards with the necessary system and on a vast scale, only if the work is done in the closest connection and intimate touch with the masses that are interested in it, and on the condition that the masses cooperate most energetically.

3. The union of any group of functions into one whole may be determined exclusively by their proximity and similarity, else there is a possibility of the least efficient combination of all or any individual branches of government activity, to the detriment of the regular development and direction of the same and to the certain amount of independence so necessary to each and every one of the activities.

4. The medico-prophylactic activity, like the entire institution for social insurance and labor safeguards, must be united, i.e., both the organizing and organic work is concentrated in the hands of bodies and institutions specially created for that purpose, and depending from the same common central body. As regards the necessary differentiation of labor it must be carried out exclusively within the common bodies, but under no circumstances must it be done by means of tearing away from them of any of the parts closely bound through common problems and peculiarities of the work, no matter how considerable each of them, taken apart, might be.

In view of the above principles, the Congress resolves that:

1. The Commissariat of Public Health must be amalgamated with the Department of Social Insurance and Labor Safeguards.

2. All organs of social insurance and labor safeguards must be built from top to bottom entirely on the basis of vocational unions' representation.

3. The question of the order of uniting the Commissariat of Public Health with the Department of Social Insurance and Labor Safeguards of the People's Commissariat of Labor is given over to the Central Executive Committee for consideration.

CULTURAL AND EDUCATIONAL WORK OF THE VOCATIONAL UNIONS AND VOCATIONAL TRAINING

(Resolution based on Tzyperovich's and Kossior's reports)

1. The Socialist revolution has put before the proletariat a series of the most important problems in the field of reconstruction. Simultaneously and in connection with the revolutionization of the economic relations, the working class, as the standard-bearer of Socialism, must get down to the work of creating a proletarian culture, instead of that of the bourgeoisie, in order to prepare the masses for the complete realization of the Socialist Commonwealth.

2. The dictatorship of the proletariat, enabling the working class to fully uti-

lize all the cultural acquisitions of mankind, is already now putting forward a new creative form of the cultural movement, in the shape of proletarian cultural organizations.

3. Vocational unions, as working class organizations, notwithstanding all their weakness and the isolation of the proletarian cultural organizations from the masses of the working class must organically enter into their work, concentrating within them all their activity for the general work along questions of science and art and endeavoring with a view to making it sound, to subject their activity to the influence and guidance of the industrially organized laboring masses.

4. The Vocational Unions are also facing as an immediate problem the utilization on as large a scale as possible of those facilities which have been created by the Commissariat of Public Education in the matter of compulsory, and free education, of education for people above school age, for technical training, etc.

The vocational unions must have their representatives in the Commissariats of Public Education, who are to shed light on the needs of the trade union movement and demand that these needs be satisfied immediately.

5. At the same time, the vocational unions are to continue their cultural and educational activity, creating educational institutions and organizations which would answer the immediate problems of the vocational movement.

6. The building up of clubs, especially for the districts and provinces, is desirable. The type of a vocational-political club is preferable, if possible of a large size.

7. It is necessary at present to build libraries in the districts. But for the central trade-industrial unions special libraries are to a certain extent superfluous (outside of special publications, guides, etc.) They can easily and with much greater success be replaced by public and municipal libraries, to which the trade-industrial unions should turn their attention, by sending to the same the representatives of their cultural-educational departments, as delegates.

8. The publishing associations of the individual unions must be technically united into one Publishing Association of the Council of Unions. The program of the publications must be adapted to the needs of the trade union movement, but at the same time it must be so flexible and elastic as to be of service to the agitational activity of the unions in various directions (appeals, bulletins, etc.). The amalgamation of the periodic trade-union organs, — is a problem of the immediate future. Besides, it is necessary to issue at present a monthly or semi-monthly magazine in order to explain the general questions of theory and practice of the trade-industrial movement.

The organization of central expeditions for all trade union publishing societies is already now an imperative necessity.

9. In order to materialize the above enumerated problems each central body of the trade-industrial unions of a given industry is to have its own cultural and educational department whose activities are to be coordinated by the Soviets (councils) of the Vocational Unions at the center and in the local branches.

On the question of vocational training the Congress finds that:

1. Vocational training, as one of the mightiest weapons in the general system of cultural-industrial socialist education of the working class, may attain its object on condition that, together with the vocational training of the workers along the lines of skilled labor, they will also be given a general industrial education, acquainting them with the general questions of the condition of technical and industrial development, political economy, economic geography, and also the questions of administrative and technical management of an enterprise.

2. Vocational training is concentrated in the hands of the Committee on Vocational Training, which is formed at the Commissariat of Public Education of the representatives of the vocational unions. The Committee is given charge of the general direction, financing and working out of a single program in the field of vocational training. For the management of each individual school a School Soviet is formed of the representatives of the vocational union, the Commissariat, and the students.

3. Within each branch of industry, a network of vocational schools is to be established as soon as the needs and requirements of the corresponding All-Russian Vocational Association are made known. In the first place the schools are being organized in those places and points for the preparation of such groups and types, of skilled workers as will be found necessary by the proper industrial associations.

4. The cultural and educational departments of the All-Russian Industrial Associations are connected with the Committee on Vocational Training of the Commissariat of Education and are to determine both the quantity and type of school needed and the technical possibility of their opening in this or that particular locality. The Committee is bound immediately to satisfy these demands, in case of necessity taking a census of the technical personnel available as instructors in vocational schools.

5. The vocational unions will utilize the schools for the organization of courses and lectures on questions of theory and practice of the labor movement, striving at their widest possible development and their transformation into a disseminator of all kinds of cultural and technical knowledge among the proletarian masses.

THE QUESTION OF PROVISIONING

(A resolution based on Comrade Antzelovich's report)

Fully supporting the general principal policy of the Workers' and Peasants' Government on the questions of provisioning and supplying the population, taking into consideration the extraordinary difficulty of the food situation, caused by the general conditions of the moment and by the weakness of the food supplying apparatus, the Congress resolves to give its best forces to the work of organization of the provisioning work, to continue the work of mobilization and centralization for this purpose of the proletarian forces on an all-Russian scale, and is hereby submitting for the approval of the Council of People's Commissaries the provisions stated below:

1. The Congress recognizes the War-Provisioning Bureau of the All-Russian

Soviet of Vocational Unions, acting in accordance with the instructions adopted by the Soviet, as the central body in charge of mobilization and distribution of the proletarian forces in the field of provisioning.

In order to fulfil its tasks the War-Provisioning Bureau of the All-Russian Soviet of Vocational Unions: (*a*) mobilizes the labor power, selecting it from among the vocational unions and their organs (the shop committees, etc.); (*b*) promotes the workers into the positions of members of the colleges, provincial provisioning committees, district provisioning committees, and other provisioning organizations, appointing them to office through the People's Commissariat for provisioning; (*c*) sends the workers' provisioning detachments composed of the best forces into the villages to do the work of organization. The detachments are working under the leadership of members delegated by the War-Provisioning Bureau into the local provisioning bodies, and are to act as auxiliary organizations to those provisioning bodies; (*d*) it organizes the provisional expeditions with special tasks to aid the provisioning organizations among them in the localities freed from occupation; (*e*) it organizes the work of labor inspection, working under the control of the War-Provisioning Bureau, both in the field of provisioning and in the allied fields of transportation, etc.; the problems of inspection consist of the renovation, reorganization and the placing of the entire system of provisioning bodies on a proletarian basis; (*f*) it selects with the aid of the proper vocational unions specialists in different lines of the provisioning work, making them available to fill executive offices; (*g*) in its work the Central War-Provisioning Bureau is leaning for support on the auxiliary local war-provisioning bureaus of the Soviets of Vocational Unions, uniting the entire activity of the vocational unions for the betterment of the provisioning work.

2. From the point of view of unity of the general system of distribution of necessaries, the Congress deems it necessary to put into practice in full measure the participation of labor cooperation in the matter of distributing the products so that, in the course of time, and labor, all the united system of distribution may be organized after the pattern of a single type of consumers' communes.

Workers' cooperative societies must become the chief distributors of products among the workers.

Considering it necessary thus to impose on the workers' cooperative societies the extremely important task of constructive Socialist work and the work of actually supplying the workers with the necessaries, without which the productivity of labor cannot be increased, the Congress holds that these functions can best be carried out by the workers' cooperatives on the following conditions: (*a*) the creation of a united organized basis for the cooperative and vocational associations (factory or mill committees), which is to be carried into practice by means of an agreement between the All-Russian Council of Vocational Unions and the All-Russian Council of Workers' Cooperative Societies; (*b*) the All-Russian Councils of Vocational Unions and the Workers' Cooperative Societies exchange representatives; (*c*) all members of the vocational unions must join the Workers' Cooperative Society and every member of the latter must become a member of a vocational union; (*d*) the common leading body of the workers' cooperative societies must be the meeting of representatives (conferences) of the shop committees and collective associations, uniting the employees and the laborers not occupied in the mills and factories; (*e*) the workers' cooperatives must immediately be induced to participate in the broadest possible manner in the work of organizing all municipal commerce; the control and general direction in the matter remaining in the hands of the provisioning bodies; (*f*) the existing special productive-distributive organs such as that in charge of transportation of the provisions, waterway transportation of provisions, (canals, rivers, etc.), must be transformed into well organized, open workers' cooperative societies; (*g*) the workers' cooperative societies are to be induced to take up the practical work of organization of these branches of industry whose scale and problems justify such work, and which are engaged in the production of the prime necessities.

3. The furnishing of the proletariat with the products provided for it by the government plans of distribution, must be insured through the appropriation of a special fund for the purpose on the plan adopted for the army. The special department of the Commissariat for Provisioning which is in charge of the planning, calculating, and distributing of the products intended for the workers, must be organized in accordance with an understanding between the All-Russian Council of Vocational Unions and the Council of Workers' Cooperatives, and it must not form its own technical and economic apparatus.

4. In order to help the methods of proletarian work to permeate more fully the entire system of the provisioning institutions it is necessary to inject into their midst representatives of Vocational Unions and Workers' Cooperative Societies, particularly representatives of the All-Russian Council of Vocational Unions and the All-Russian Council of Cooperative Societies, into the Collegium of the People's Commissariat for Provisioning.

In the matter of preparing the products which are subject to monopoly, by government counter-agents (as per decree of January 21st) the central workers' cooperatives (city) and all centralized workers' cooperative organizations (regional, provincial and all-Russian) are to be called upon to help, while the matter of preparing the products not subject to monopoly should be entirely given over to the cooperative societies, headed by the Workers' Cooperative Society, the management to be given over to the Central Buying Committee (Tzentrozakup) and a corresponding portion of the products is to be set aside for the needs of the army.

5. In order to create a solid basis in the matter of supplying farm products and with a view to intensifying agriculture and other types of farming it is necessary to call upon the workers' cooperative societies to properly utilize and organize the large Soviet agricultural establishments and other farming undertakings.

6. For the successful solution of its tasks in the domain of Socialist construction work it is necessary to bring about the closest organizational union and coordination of activity of the vocational unions and workers' cooperative societies in the matter of raising the class consciousness of that proletariat and, for this purpose, the joint organization of workers' homes, clubs, institutes for practitioners, and so on.

THE QUESTION OF ORGANIZATION

(Resolution based an M. Tomsky's report)

1.
GENERAL PRINCIPLES

1. Adapting its organizations to the conditions of the economic struggle in capitalist society, the working class in the interests of economy and concentration of its divided forces, gradually passed over from the close narrow guild organizations to the broader vocational and, finally, in the course of struggle against capitalism, building its forces on the principle of more efficient centralization of power for the realization of its war aims (class war aims), it came to form organizations embracing all the workers of a given branch of industry (production) into one union.

The industrial union is one union having the follow-lowing basic characteristics: (*a*) the union rallies all the workers and other employees engaged in a given branch of production, regardless of his functions; (*b*) the treasury is centralized; (*c*) the business of the union is transacted on the basis of democratic centralization; (*d*) the wage scales and conditions of labor are determined by one central body for all the categories of labor; (*e*) a uniform principle of construction from top to bottom; (*f*) the sections are playing the part of technical and auxiliary organs; (*g*) the interests of the industrially organized workers and other employees of a given industry are represented before the outside world by one central body.

2. The industrial union comprises only the permanent workers and employees of a given industry who are directly engaged in the process of production or serve to aid the same. All auxiliary branches serving *not production but the producers* and all the temporary and casual help remain members of their industrial union.

3. This principle of construction of our unions recognized by the third Conference of the Vocational Unions, and by the first All-Russian Congress of Vocational Unions, presupposing the union of all the workers of a given industry into one organization (union), can be consistently carried into practice only by means of uniting all the workers and employees ("higher" and "lower") into one union, which became possible of realization only after the political and economic prejudices separating the laborer from the other employees and from the technical personnel have been done away with.

4. Even if the first Congress of Vocational Unions considered it impracticable to unite into one union all the higher employees and laborers,—at the present moment, after a year of proletarian dictatorship during which a good deal of the antagonism between the different categories of laborers and other employees has been spent, when it has been proved from experience that one union in its turn leads to the eradication of all antagonism in the midst of the workers—it must now be recognized as desirable and necessary to unite into one union all persons who are wage workers engaged in one establishment, one industry or one institution.

Only in such establishments or institutions where the hiring of laborers and other employees and the increase or decrease of their wages is being decided by one member of the administrative or technical personnel, the latter cannot be members of the given union.

5. The industrial principle of union structure as applied to workers occupied in other branches of national industries, than manufacture (transportation, commerce, and farming), and also in institutions fulfilling definite functions of government (postal-telegraph, medico-sanitary departments, education, etc.), must be used to unite the workers of small isolated branches of industry and management into more powerful unions. As a basis for such amalgamation one must take the similarity of conditions of labor and the functions carried out.

6. Categorically defending the consistent introduction and application of the principle underlying production as regards all categories of workers, not accepting into its labor organizations those unions which are built on guild, corporation and narrow trade lines, for the purpose of better serving the economic interests of the most typical industrial groups and categories, the organization of sections on a local and national scale is allowed within each vocational union.

The unions binding together several allied branches of industry have the right to form industrial sections, the same having the right to call independent Congresses in order to decide the questions of their own industry, on condition however, that the decisions of such sectional Congresses, which will be contrary to the rulings of the general Congress or the regulations of the leading organs of the labor union movement, may be annulled by the leading body of the industrial union.

7. Striving towards unity and smooth work in labor union activity and the greatest efficiency in the utilization of the power and means at the disposal of the labor unions, it is necessary to recognize most definitely the principle of centralization of the union organization, based on unity and centralization of union finances and strict inter- and intra-union discipline.

8. With this principle as a starting-point, the *organization of the section cannot have the character of open or masked federalism.* Under no circumstances could the sections be allowed to have separate sectional treasuries, additional assessment of members of the sections for organization and agitation and generally for any work of the union, neither can they be allowed independent representation outside of the union or to build the leading union organs, committees, on the principle of sectional representation.

9. In exceptional cases of reconstruction of the existing federated unions into a centralized industrial union, only as an allowance for the transitional stage the Executive Committee elected at the meeting of all the delegates or at the meeting of the All-Russian Congress, can be enlarged through the addition of representatives of the sections, who then have no vote, only a voice.

10. All attempts to violate the principle of industrial organization for the purpose of restoring the federated trade unions by means of organization of the inter-sectional bureaus uniting analogous sections of the various industrial unions, must be emphatically condemned.

11. Fighting for the complete annihilation of classes, at this transitional period of proletarian dictatorship, the Russian trade-union movement aiming at the union of all workers into centralized industrial unions for the purpose of subjecting the semi-proletarian elements to the influence of the economically organized proletariat and inducing it to enter the class struggle and take part in Socialist reconstruction; we think it necessary to get the new, and as yet unorganized, strata of government and social workers to join the All-Russian Vocational Associations, on condition of their complete submission to proletarian discipline and to all regulations of the leading central bodies of the trade union movement, and particularly, the principles of organization.

12. At the same time it would be the greatest error at the present stage of development of our trade union movement with its insufficient degree of organization, to infuse into it the craftsmen and small shop owners who due to their isolation and unorganized state, do not allow of proletarian control; the same applies to the labor "artels," "unions of labor communes" and so-called professional people who are not wage workers.

Being the representatives of the dying crafts and petty bourgeois industry, these elements permeated with the conservative economic ideology of individual and small-scale production (artel), due to their numerical size, are liable to disorganize the ranks of the economically organized proletariat.

13. Considering as the only correct and fundamental basis for the union of the workers into industrial unions, the economic basis (the economic part played by the groups of laborers in the general system of national economy), the All-Russian Vocational Association cannot accept into its midst unions *built along national, religious, and generally, any unions not built along economic lines.*

14. Uniting the laborers and other employees into unions, independently of their political and religious beliefs, the Russian trade union movement as a whole, taking the position of the international class struggle, resolutely condemns the idea of neutralism, and considers it a prerequisite for the admission of individual unions into the all-Russian and local associations—that they recognize the revolutionary class struggle for the realization of socialism *by means of the dictatorship of the proletariat.*

15. Regarding the Russian labor-union movement as one close proletarian class organization, having one common class aim—to win and organize the socialist system, one must admit that *any member of any industrial union*, affiliated with the all-Russian or local union council, who is fulfilling his duties as such, being at the same time a member of the All-Russian General Vocational Association, upon being transferred from one industry to another, *joins the proper union with the rights of an old member*, without paying any initiation fee. No one must be at the same time a member of two unions.

16. This latter rule wholly applies also to the group transfer of whole establishments from one union to another—*no payments are to be made out of the treasury of the unions, nor are to be made either to the members who leave it or to the union into which they are transferred*, by the first union.

17. Endeavoring to better the economic conditions of all the workers, regardless of whether they are members of the union or not, the unions taking upon themselves the responsibility for the proper functioning of an establishment or institution, for the labor discipline among the workers and the enforcement of the union regulations of wages and standards of production, the unions must endeavor *to introduce compulsory membership* in all the establishments and institutions entering into it, *through resolutions adopted at general meetings of the workers.*

18. Recognizing *the necessity of a united plan for the construction of all trade unions* as the only condition insuring right relations between the individual local organizations and their centers, also insuring the enforcement of union regulations and union discipline, the second Congress thinks it necessary, for the purpose of creating unity of activity on a local as well as national scale, to adopt a united scheme for the structure of the industrial unions and their combines.

2.
THE STRUCTURE OF THE TRADE UNIONS AND SOVIETS:

1. The highest directing body of the all-Russian labor union movement is the All-Russian Congress of Trade Unions and the All-Russian Central Soviet of Vocational Unions operating from one Congress to the other, on the basis of principle regulations adopted by the Congress.

> *Note.* A conference is called only in case it is impossible to call
> a properly organized congress.

2. All regulations of the All-Russian Congresses, Conferences and the All-Russian Central Council of the Industrial Unions are compulsory not only to all the unions, affiliated with the All-Russian Vocational Association, but for every individual member of a union, as well.

3. *Violation of the rules and disregard of the same on the part of individual unions* carries with it expulsion of such a union from the family of the proletarian unions.

4. The supreme organ of the All-Russian Industrial Union is its Central Committee; all rulings of that committee which do not contradict the regulations issued by the higher councils of the All-Russian General Vocational Association are obligatory for all of its branches and for each and every one of its members.

5. All local councils of the unions are being constructed according to the plan of the All-Russian Central Council of the Vocational Unions, with a corresponding proportional change of numerical ratio. All congresses of vocational unions are being called on the principle of direct proportion.

6. The rulings of the All-Russian Industrial Unions cannot be nullified by the rulings of the local councils of unions and are obligatory for the organs of the given union in each locality.

7. The local councils of the Vocational Unions being the leading organs of the labor union movement and authorized representatives of the entire proletariat, economically organized within a certain locality, are at the same time guided in their activities by all the rules of the All-Russian Congresses, Conferences and the

All-Russian Central Council of the Trade-Industrial Unions, and as regards the branches of the industrial unions, the regulations laid down by their guiding central bodies are obligatory. The rulings of the local Trade Union Councils which are in contradiction to the regulations of the policy of the entire unions or their managing bodies, are not obligatory for the local branches of the industrial unions.

8. The branches of the All-Russian Industrial Unions affiliated with the All-Russian Central Trade Unions Council automatically enter into the local Trade Union Councils.

9. The local Trade Union Councils are to see to it that the unions are properly organized, and that they follow the directions issued by the governing bodies and fulfil their financial obligations towards the unions; they are also to aid and support them in their activities.

10. In the interests of centralization of union activity, the strengthening of the ties between the centers and the local bodies, and in order to place the finances of the unions on a proper plane and bring about closer cooperation and connection between the trade unions on the one hand, and the organs of the Supreme Council of National Economy and the Commissariat of Labor, on the other, in the work of bringing about a uniform structure of the Trade Unions and Union Councils and standardizing the wage scales throughout the country,—one must admit that the geographical (provincial) amalgamations as well as the provincial Union Councils are only unnecessary organs of transmission between the center and the periphery which constitute a nonproductive expenditure of energy and means.

11. The All-Russian Centers, their branches and subdivisions in the various localities, united through the Trade Union Councils, constructed after the pattern of the All-Russian Central Trade Union Council, the Shop Committees or Employees' Associations (Collective Associations) as the original *nuclei* of the trade unions— this is the best scheme of organization structure, answering the basic problems at the present moment confronting the trade union movement. Territorial grouping according to divisions and subdivisions should be established by the All-Russian Central body of the given union, depending upon the geographical area and degree of concentration of any given branch of industry, keeping, insofar as possible within the boundaries fixed by the administrative divisions.

Only by observing the given scheme of organization can the finances of the union be placed on a proper level and the centers receive due financial strength, which is a necessary condition for further and more systematic activity.

12. The most suitable principle by which to determine the membership dues during the period of chronic depreciation of paper money would be a proportional assessment. The normal amount of membership dues, the Congress considers is one per cent of the wages earned. Special additional dues or assessments for special needs of the local divisions of the industrial unions are allowed only upon the resolution of general meetings, or meetings of delegates or conferences of a given union.

13. Regarding the Branch of the Industrial Union (within a province or region) as the highest organ of the union in the given locality (government or region), as

the first step toward the actual realization of the centralization of the union funds, the Congress considers the following financial relations as necessary:

(*a*) Fifty per cent of all membership dues of the branches of the All-Russian Central Industrial Union go to the All-Russian Central Committee of the given Industrial Union.

(*b*) The divisions (district and sub-regional) of a branch (government or region) of a Union work according to the budget approved by the latter.

(*c*) Ten per cent of all the funds remaining at the disposal of a branch of a union goes to the local Trade Union Council.

(*d*) The local bureaus of the Trade Unions (in small towns) exist on 10 per cent of the budget appropriated by the branch of the industrial union to its divisions.

(*e*) The local unions which are not affiliated with any all-Russian union associations are to give 10 per cent to the local Trade Union Council, and 10 per cent to the All-Russian Central Trade Union Council transferred through the local Trade Union Council.

14. All trade organizations as well as members who have not met their financial obligations within three months without sufficient reasons, are automatically expelled from their union and from the All-Russian Trade Association, and can be reinstated only upon payment of the sum they owe plus the usual initiation fee.

15. The following initiation fees are to be fixed: (*a*) half a day's wages for individual members entering the union, (*b*) the All-Russian Trade Union upon entering the All-Russian Central Trade Union Council pays 10 per cent of all the initiation fees collected from the total number of its members, (*c*) the same amount is paid by all the branches of the All-Russian Trade Unions upon their admission into the local Trade Union Council, (*d*) the local unions which have no all-Russian trade union pay upon entering the local council 10 per cent of the initiation fees collected, a half of which amount goes to the All-Russian Central Trade Union Council.

16. In the interests of the development of union activity with the present character of the Russian trade union movement, all special funds which cannot be touched, such as the strike fund, the reserve funds, etc., must be annulled as such and added to the rest of the union's general treasury. The fund for the aid of unions outside of Soviet Russia is being created by the All-Russian Central Trade Union Council for which purpose special collections and contributions are to be used.

17. In the interests of the proper arrangement of the control system, the simplification and systematization of the union's business, we must make it obligatory to have a single uniform system, as worked out by the All-Russian Central Trade Union Council.

18. The basic nucleus of the Industrial Union on the spot is the Factory Committee or the Collective Association of the office employees in the form of an Office

Workers' Union.

19. "Regulations of the Factory and Mill Committees" adopted by the Moscow Trade Union Council and approved by the All-Russian Central Council of the Industrial Unions coordinated with the resolutions of the present second All-Russian Congress of Trade Unions must be used as the basis for the determination of the part, the tasks and interrelations of the Factory and Mill Committees with the other organizations.

20. As a basis for the regulations governing the Employees' Associations (Collective Associations), in addition to the general principles which form the basis of the "Factory and Mill Committee Regulations," the following principles are to be laid down:

> (*a*) Participation in the hiring and dismissal of employees, (*b*) obligatory participation in the Wage Scale Committees and endeavor to see to it that the wage scale regulations be carried out in practice, (*c*) the recognition of the collective association and its rights to exist only as an organ of the corresponding union, (*d*) participation in the organization and improvement of the technical apparatus of the given institution, (*e*) non-interference with the general direction of the activities of the state and social institutions.

The All-Russian Central Trade Union Council is authorized within the shortest time to work out and publish the regulations of the Factory and Mill Committees and the Employees' Collective Associations.

21. To avoid mixing up of terms and ideas regarding the character of the union organs we must recognize the uniform terminology of the same, as carrying out the same functions, namely:

> (*a*) All-Russian Central Trade Union Council retains its name, (*b*) the leading organs of the All-Russian Trade Unions are called "Central Committee of the Trade Unions," their executive organs are to be called: "Presidium of the Central Committee of the Trade Unions," (*c*) their government (province) organs—"The management of the government (province) or regional branch of the All-Russian Trade Union," (*d*) the Local Government Trade Union Councils are called: "Such and such Government Trade Union Council," and the district councils as well as the small town councils "Such and such District Trade Union Bureau," "Such and such Trade Union Bureau."

22. All-Russian Central Trade Union Council on the basis of the principles laid down, must work out in the shortest possible period the following sample by-laws which are to be obligatory for all trade organizations affiliated with any of the following All-Russian Trade Associations:

> (*a*) The All-Russian Trade Union, (*b*) local union having no corresponding all-Russian association, (*c*) Local Trade Union

Council, (*d*) Trade Union Bureau.

23. The All-Russian Central Trade Union Council must work out and enact through the People's Commissariat of Labor and the Soviet of National Economy or the All-Russian Central Executive Committee, the regulations governing the coalitions on the following basis: (*a*) the right to be called a union is given only to trade unions affiliated with the All-Russian Central Trade Union Council, registered and published by the latter, (*b*) all other organizations of an economic character not affiliated with the All-Russian Trade Association are to be called "societies."

24. The All-Russian Central Trade Union Council and the government councils must periodically report on all unions registered with it.

25. In accordance with the general principles of organization, adopted at the second Trade Union Congress the corresponding amendments are to be introduced into the by-laws of the All-Russian Central Trade Union Council adopted by the first All-Russian Trade Union Congress.

BY-LAWS OF THE ALL-RUSSIAN CENTRAL TRADES UNION COUNCIL

(Amended and approved by the Congress)

1. The All-Russian Trade Union Congress elects an executive body of the All-Russian Central Trades Union Council—the presiding officers (Presidium), who are to submit a detailed report on their activity to the following Congress.

2. The supreme leading body of the All-Russian Trade-Union Association is the All-Russian Central Trade-Union Council, which is to be guided in its activity by resolutions of congresses and conferences and which is responsible for its actions to the All-Russian Trades Union Congress.

3. All the regulations of the All-Russian Congresses, Conferences as well as those passed by the All-Russian Central Trades Union Council are obligatory to all unions affiliated with the All-Russian Trades Union Association as well as to every union member. The violation of these rules and disobedience of the same carries with it expulsion from the family of proletarian unions.

4. The All-Russian Central Council is to fulfil the following tasks:

> (*a.*) It is to maintain and establish a connection with all the existing and newly arising trade union organizations;

> (*b.*) It is to aid in the creation of local all-Russian vocational unions as well as the amalgamation of all trades;

> (*c.*) It is to establish connections with the central trade union bodies of all countries;

> (*d.*) It is to carry out all the necessary work connected with the preparation and calling of All-Russian conferences and congresses, it works out a program of business to be transacted by

the congresses, it takes care of the preparation of reports, and it publishes the fundamental principles;

(*e.*) It appoints the time for the calling of conferences and congresses;

(*f.*) It periodically publishes in the press reports on its activities;

(*g.*) It issues its bulletin (periodical organ);

(*h.*) It connects, and acts as representative for the entire trade-union movement before the Central government institutions and social organizations;

(*i.*) It aids the unions in their work of organization and guides that work, for which purpose it issues various by-laws, instructions, forms of accounting (book-keeping), etc.;

(*j.*) It takes part in organizations and institutions, serving the interests of cultural and educational activity among the proletariat;

(*k.*) It aids in promoting the development of the trade union movement, by means of verbal and written propaganda and agitation.

6. In order to accomplish its tasks successfully, the All-Russian Central Trades Union Council organizes the necessary departments.

7. The funds of the All-Russian Central Trades-Union Council consist of the following: (*a*) 10 per cent of the membership dues collected by the Central Committees of the All-Russian Trade Union Association; (*b*) five per cent of the revenue coming from the local unions not affiliated with the All-Russian Trade Unions, but affiliated, through the local Soviet, with the All-Russian All-Trades Association, (*c*) out of appropriations designated by the organs of the Soviet Government for specific purposes.

8. The All-Russian Central Trade Union Council is composed of the following:

(*a*) Nine members elected by the Congress, and

(*b*) Representatives of the All-Russian Trade Unions, on the basis of one delegate to every 30,000 to 50,000 workers, and one more delegate to every additional 50,000 dues-paying members.

Note. All-Russian Trades Unions whose membership is below 30,000, send their representative, who has a voice, but no vote. Unions whose dues-paying membership is below 30,000 may unite and send a delegate to the All-Russian Trades Union Council, who will then have the right to vote at the meetings.

9. The nine members elected by the congress are to be the presiding officers of the All-Russian Central Council; in order to effect a change in the composition of the presidium, a vote of not less than two-thirds of the general number of members of the All-Russian Central Council is required, or if the All-Russian Associations

demand the recall of that body, the total membership of the associations demanding such recall must exceed one-half of the entire membership of the All-Russian Association comprising all trades.

Note. The members of the presidium (executive committee), are to be replaced (in case they resign or are recalled) at the plenary session of the All-Russian Central Trade Union Council.

10. Such recall and election of a new executive body may take place only in extraordinary cases when the general conditions do not permit the calling of an extraordinary congress or conference.

11. A plenary session of the All-Russian Central Council takes place at least once a month. The All-Russian Central Council at a meeting of all its members elects an auditing committee and other committees and responsible officers, leaving to the executive committee (presiding officers) to organize branches (departments), to invite workers to join them, etc.

12. The All-Russian Conference of Trades-Unions is to consist of all the members of the council (Soviet), and of representatives of provincial trades-union councils—one to every 25,000 members.

Note. Representatives of All-Russian Associations who are admitted to the plenary session (*plenum*) with only a voice and no vote, have the right to vote at the conference.

13. The All-Russian Central Trades Union calls congresses of the trades unions at intervals not longer than one year. Extraordinary congresses are called at the decision of the All-Russian Central Council, at the demand of All-Russian Associations, or in cases where the All-Russian Associations having not less than half the total membership affiliated with the All-Russian Workmen's Association, demand that an extraordinary convention be called.

14. The right to representation at the Trades-Union Congresses is restricted to those unions which in their activity are guided by the principles of the international class struggle of the proletariat, which are affiliated with the local councils of the trades unions and which pay their dues regularly.

15. The following have a right to vote at the congress:

(*a*) The local trades unions having a dues-paying membership of no less than 3,000, are entitled to one delegate, and those whose membership exceeds 5,000 are entitled to one delegate for every 5,000 dues-paying members (complete 5,000 only, not for any fraction thereof).

(*b*) The central All-Russian Associations are entitled to one delegate each; but in case the total number of workers affiliated with them exceeds 10,000 they are entitled to two delegates.

(*c*) Petrograd and Moscow send three delegates each.

(*d*) Local unions having under 3,000 members may amalgamate for the purpose of sending their delegates.

16. The following have a voice, but no vote:

(*a*) Representatives of the central bodies of Socialist parties; of the All-Russian Central Executive Committee of the Council (Soviet) of Workers' and Peasants' Delegates; individuals and institutions at the invitation of the All-Russian Central Council or the Congress itself.

(*b*) All members of the All-Russian Central Soviet.

17. The rules of procedure for the congress (convention) are worked out by the All-Russian Central Council and are subject to approval by the congress.

18. The order of business (program) to be transacted at the convention is to be made public at least one month before the congress is convened. Individual organizations have the right to introduce new points into the order of business not later than two weeks prior to the meeting of the congress, of which changes the All-Russian Central Council immediately notifies, through the press, all the trades unions.

ORDER OF ADMISSION OF ALL-RUSSIAN TRADES UNIONS INTO THE ALL-RUSSIAN CENTRAL TRADES UNIONS COUNCIL

19. An All-Russian Trades Union, desiring to enter the All-Trade Association must submit to the presidium of the All-Russian Central Trades Union Council the following documents:

(*a*) the by-laws,

(*b*) information on the number of dues-paying members,

(*c*) information on the existing branches and number of dues-paying members of each of them,

(*d*) minutes of any convention or conference at which the central committee of the organization has been elected,

(*e*) financial report,

(*f*) sample copies of such publications as the All-Russian Trades Union has published, and all other material shedding light on the character of the union's works.

20. An All-Russian Trades Union may be registered with, and admitted into, the All-Russian Central Trades Union Council on the following conditions:

(*a*) the by-laws and the structure of the union are to be brought into accord with the general principles of organization as adopted by the convention and carried out by the All-Russian Central Trades Union Council;

(*b*) the character and activity of the union must not contradict the resolutions of the All-Russian Trades Union Convention or the general tendencies of the Russian trades union movement;

(*c*) the payment of a corresponding initiation fee;

21. An all-Russian union may be expelled at a plenary session from the All-Russian Central Trades Union Council on the following grounds:

(*a*) failure to obey the general rules of discipline obligatory to all trades union organizations;

(*b*) failure to pay membership dues within three months, without any reasonable cause.

22. The All-Russian Central Trades Union Council, in cases where the central committee of the All-Russian Trades Union violates the decisions of the convention, conference, or All-Russian Central Trades Union Council, may dissolve the same, and must immediately call an All-Russian convention or conference of the given trades union for the purpose of electing a new directing body.

November 7, 1919.

THE FINANCIAL POLICY AND THE RESULTS OF THE ACTIVITIES OF THE PEOPLE'S COMMISSARIAT OF FINANCE
(1917–1919)

I

When the Soviet Government was first organized, a number of purely financial questions arose which necessitated the utilization of the services of the old financial-administrative apparatus in the form in which it existed prior to the October Revolution. It is quite natural that the first period of work in the domain of finance, that is, between the October Revolution and the Brest-Litovsk Peace, had of necessity to be marked by efforts to conquer the financial apparatus, its central as well as its local bodies, to make a study of its own functions and, somehow or other, to adapt itself to the requirements of the time.

While in the domain of the Soviet Government's economic and general policy, this period has been marked by two most far-reaching and important changes which, strictly speaking, had been prepared prior to the October Revolution—the nationalization of banks and the annulment of the government debt; the financial policy, in the narrow sense of the word, did not disclose any new departures, not even the beginnings of original constructive work.

Gradually taking over the semi-ruined pre-revolutionary financial apparatus, however, the Soviet Government was compelled to adopt measures for the systematization of the country's finances in their entirety.

This second period in the work of the People's Commissariat for Finances (approximately up to August, 1918) also fails to show any features of sharply marked revolutionary change. From the very beginning the authorities have been confronted with a chaotic condition of the country's financial affairs. All this, in connection with the large deficit which became apparent in the state budget, compelled the

Commissariat of Finance to concentrate its immediate attention on straightening the general run of things and, thus, prepare the ground for further reforms.

In order to accomplish the systematizing of the financial structure, the Government had to lean for support on the already existing unreformed institutions, i.e., the central department of finance, the local administrative-financial organs—the fiscal boards tax inspection, treasuries, excise boards—and, more particularly, the financial organs of the former local institutions for self-government (Zemstvos, and municipalities).

Such a plan of work seemed most feasible, since the apparatus appeared suitable for fulfilling slightly modified functions; but the local government was not yet sufficiently crystallized or firmly established, neither was any stable connection established between that local government and the central bodies.

Under such circumstances, the old institutions, which by force of habit continued to work exclusively at the dictate of and in accordance with instructions from the central bodies, seemed to be the most convenient and efficient means of carrying out measures which the central authorities had planned to straighten out the general disorder prevailing in financial affairs.

However, this idea soon had to be discarded, the local Soviets insofar as they organized themselves and put their executive organs into definite shape, could not and did not have the right to neglect the work of the old financial organs functioning in the various localities, since the Soviets represented the local organs of the central government as a whole, and since it was upon them that the responsibility for all the work done in the localities, rested.

Under such conditions friction was inevitable. In accordance with the principles of the old bureaucratic order, the local financial institutions neither knew nor had any idea of subordination other than the slavish subordination to the central authorities which excluded all initiative on their part.

Under the new conditions, these local financial institutions were to constitute only a small component part of the local Soviets. Acute misunderstanding of the local authorities among themselves and between the local and central authorities on the subject of interrelations among all of these institutions, have demonstrated the imperative necessity for a reorganization. With this work of reforming the local financial organs (September, 1918) a new period opened: the third period in the activity of the commissariat, which coincides with the gradual strengthening of the general course of our economic policy. The economic policy definitely and decisively occupies the first place which duly belongs to it, while the financial policy, insofar as it is closely bound up with the economic policy, is being regulated and directed in accordance with the general requirements of the latter.

II

The financial policy of Soviet Russia was, for the first time, definitely outlined by the eighth (March, 1919) Convention of the Russian Communist Party.

The eighth party convention clearly and concretely stated our financial problems for the transitionary period, and now our task consists in seeing to it that the work of the financial organs of the Republic should be in accord with the principles accepted by the party.

These principles, briefly, are as follows: (1) Soviet Government State monopoly of the banking institutions; (2) radical reconstruction and simplifications of the banking operations, by means of transforming the banking apparatus into one of uniform accounting and general bookkeeping for the Soviet Republic; (3) the enactment of measures widening the sphere of accounting without the medium of money, with the final object of total elimination of money; (4) and, in view of the transformation of the government power into an organization fulfilling the functions of economic management for the entire country,—the transformation of the pre-revolutionary state budget into the budget of the economic life of the nation as a whole.

In regard to the necessity for covering the expenses of the functioning state apparatus during the period of transition, the program adopted outlines the following plan: "The Russian Communist Party will advocate the transition from the system of levying contributions from the capitalists, to a proportional income and property tax: and, insofar as this tax outlives itself, due to the widely applied expropriation of the propertied classes, the government expenditures must be covered by the immediate conversion of part of the income derived from the various state monopolies into government revenue."

In short, we arrive at the conclusion that no purely financial policy, in its pre-revolutionary sense of independence and priority, can or ought to exist in Soviet Russia. The financial policy plays a subsidiary part, for it depends directly upon the economic policy and upon the changes which occur in the various phases of Russia's political and economic order.

During the transitional period from capitalism to Socialism the government concentrates all of its attention on the organization of industry and on the activities of the organs for exchange and distribution of commodities.

The financial apparatus is an apparatus subsidiary to the organs of production and distribution of merchandise. During the whole of this transitional period the financial administration is confronted with the following task: (1) supplying the productive and distributive organs with money, as a medium of exchange, not even abolished by economic evolution, and (2) the formation of an accounting system, with the aid of which the government materialize the exchange and distribution of products. Finally, since all the practical work in the domain of national and financial economy cannot and should not proceed otherwise than in accordance with a strictly defined plan, it is the function of the financial administration to create and compile the state budget in such a manner that it might approximate as closely as possible the budget of the entire national economic life.

In addition to this, one of the largest problems of the Commissariat of Finance was the radical reform of the entire administration of the Department of Finance, from top to bottom, in such a manner that the fundamental need of the moment would be realized most fully—the realization of the dictatorship of the proletariat and the poorest peasantry in the financial sphere.

III

The work of the financial institutions for the solution of the first problem of our financial policy, i.e., the monopolization of the entire banking business in the hands of the Soviet Government, may be considered as having been completed during the past year.

The private commercial banks were nationalized on December 14, 1917, but even after this act there still remained a number of private credit institutions. Among these foremost was the "Moscow People's Bank" (Moscow Narodny Bank) a so-called cooperative institution. There were also societies for mutual credit, foreign banks (Lion Credit Warsaw Bank, Caucasian Bank, etc.); and private land banks, city and government (provisional) credit associations.

Finally, together with the Moscow People's Bank there existed government institutions—savings banks, and treasuries. A number of measures were required to do away with that lack of uniformity involved and to prepare the ground for the formation of a uniform accounting system.

A number of decrees of the Soviet of People's Commissaries and regulations issued by the People's Commissariat of Finance, have completed all this work from September 1918 to May 1919.

By a decree of October 10th, 1918, the Societies for Mutual Credit were liquidated; three decrees of December 2nd, 1918, liquidated the foreign banks, regulated the nationalization of the Moscow People's (Cooperative) Bank and the liquidation of the municipal banks; and, finally, on May 17th, 1919, the city and state Mutual Credit Associations were liquidated. As regards the question of consolidating the treasuries with the offices of the People's Bank, this has been provided in a decree issued on October 31st, 1918; the amalgamation of the savings banks with the People's Bank has been affected on April 10th, 1918.

Thus, with the issuance of all the above-mentioned decrees, all the private credit associations have been eliminated and all existing Government Credit Institutions have been consolidated into one People's Bank of the Russian Republic. The last step in the process of reform was the decree of the People's Commissariat of Finance which consolidated the State Treasury Department with the central administration of the People's Bank. This made possible, by uniting the administration of these organs, the enforcement of the decree concerning the amalgamation of the treasuries with the People's Bank. The decree of the People's Commissariat of Finance of October 29th, 1918, issued pursuant to Section 902 of rules on state and county financial organs, practically ends the entire reform of uniting the treasuries with the institutions of the Bank.

This reform constitutes the greatest revolutionary departure, in strict accordance with the instructions contained in the party program. Prior to the completion of this reform, the old pre-revolutionary principle continued to prevail—that of opposition of the State Treasury to the State Bank, which was independent financially, having its own means, operating at the expense of its capital stock, and acting as a depository for the funds of the State Treasury and as its creditor. Insofar as the new scheme of our financial life has been realized, this dualism, has finally disappeared in the process of realization of the reform. The Bank has now actually become the only budget-auditing savings account machinery of the Russian Socialist Federal Soviet Republic. At the present moment it is serving all the departments of the state administration, in the sense that it meets all the government expenditures and receives all the state revenue. It takes care of all accounting between the governmental institutions, on the one hand, and the private establishments and individuals on the other. Through the hands of the People's Bank pass all the budgets of all institutions and enterprises, even the state budget itself; in it is concentrated the central bookkeeping which is to unify all the operations and to give a general picture of the national economic balance.

Thus, we may consider that the fundamental work, i.e., "the monopolization of the entire banking business in the hands of the Soviet Government, the radical alteration and the simplification of banking operations by means of converting the banking apparatus into an apparatus for uniform accounting and general bookkeeping of the Soviet Republic"—has been accomplished by the Commissariat of Finance.

IV

As regards the carrying into practice of a number of measures intended to widen the sphere of accounting without the aid of money, the Commissariat of Finance has, during the period above referred to, undertaken some steps insofar as this was possible under the circumstances.

As long as the state did not overcome the shortage of manufactured articles, caused by the general dislocation of industrial life, and as long as it could arrange for a moneyless direct exchange of commodities with the villages, nothing else remains for it than to take, insofar as possible, all possible steps to reduce the instances where money is used as a medium of exchange. Through an increase of moneyless operations between the departments, and between the government and individuals, economically dependent upon it, the ground is prepared for the abolition of money.

The first step in this direction was the decree of the Soviet of People's Commissaries of January 23rd, 1919, on accounting operations, containing regulations on the settling of merchandise accounts (products, raw material, manufactured articles, etc.) among Soviet institutions, and also among such industrial and commercial establishments as have been nationalized, taken over by the municipalities, or are under the control of the Supreme Council of National Economy, the People's Commissariat for Food Supply, and Provincial Councils of National Economy and their sub-divisions.

In accordance with this decree, the above-mentioned accounts are to be settled without the medium of currency, by means of a draft upon the state treasury for the amount chargeable to the consuming institution, and to be credited to the producing institution, or enterprise. In the strict sense, the decree establishes a principle, in accordance with which any Soviet institution or governmental enterprise requiring merchandise, must not resort to the aid of private dealers, but is in duty bound to apply to the corresponding Soviet institutions, accounting, producing or distributing those articles. Thus, it was proposed, by means of the above-mentioned decree, to reduce an enormous part of the state budget to the mere calculation of interdepartmental accounts, income on one side and expenditures on the other. In other words, it becomes possible to transact an enormous part of the operations without the use of money as a medium of exchange.

As regards the policy of the Commissariat of Finance in the domain of the circulation of money, one of the most important measures in this respect was the decree of the Soviet of People's Commissaries of May 15th, 1919, on the issue of new paper money of the 1918 type.

This decree states the following motive for the issue of new money: "this money is being issued with the object of gradually replacing the paper money now in circulation of the present model, the form of which in no way corresponds to the foundations of Russia's new political order, and also for the purpose of driving out of circulation various substitutes for money which have been issued due to the shortage of paper money."

The simultaneous issue of money of the old and new type made it impossible for the Commissariat of Finance to immediately commence the exchange of money, but this in no way did or does prevent it from preparing the ground for such exchange, in connection with the annulment of the major part of the old money in a somewhat different manner. Creating a considerable supply of money of the new model (1918) and increasing the productivity of the currency printing office, the Commissariat is to gradually pass over to, in fact has already begun, the issue of money exclusively of the new type. A little while after the old paper money has ceased to be printed, the laboring population, both rural and urban, as well as the Red Guards all of whom are not in position to accumulate large sums, will soon have none of the old money. Then will be the time to annul the money of the old type, since this annulment will not carry with it any serious encroachment on the interests of the large laboring masses.

Thus the issue of new money is one of the most needed first steps on the road to the preparation of the fundamental problem, that is the annihilation of a considerable quantity of money of the old type, reducing in this way the general volume of the mass of paper money in circulation.

We thus see that here, too, the Commissariat of Finance followed a definite policy. It goes without saying that from the point of view of Socialist policy all measures in the domain of money circulation are mere palliative measures. The Commissariat of Finance entertains no doubts as to the fact that a radical solution of the question is possible only by eliminating money as a medium of exchange.

The most immediate problem before the Commissariat of Finance is undoubtedly the accomplishment of the process which has already begun, namely, the selection of the most convenient moment for the annulment of the old money. As regards the part which currency generally (at this moment of transition) plays, there can be no doubt that now it is the only and therefore inevitable system of financing the entire governmental machinery and that the choice of other ways in this direction entirely depends upon purely economic conditions, i.e., mainly upon the process of organization and restoration of the national economy as a whole.

V

The explanatory note, attached to the budget for July to December, 1918, thus depicts our future budget: "When the Socialist reconstruction of Russia has been completed, when all the factories, mills and other establishments have passed into the hands of the government, and the products of these will go to the government freely and directly, when the agricultural and farming products will also freely flow into the government stores either in exchange for manufactured articles or as duty in kind ... then the state budget will reflect not the condition of the monetary transactions of the State Treasury ... but the condition of the operations involving material values, belonging to the State, and the operations will be transacted without the aid of money, at any rate without money in its present form."

It is clear that at present the conditions are not yet fully prepared for the transition to the above-stated new form of state budget. But, in spite of this, the Commissariat of Finance has taken a big step forward in the direction of reforming our budget.

The budget of the Russian Socialist Federal Soviet Republic, adopted by the All-Russian Central Executive Committee on May 20, 1919, represents the experiment in effecting a survey not so much of the financial activity of the state, as of its economic activity, even though it is as yet in the form of money.

In the work of reforming the budget, the Commissariat of Finance has come across two obstacles which are a heritage of the pre-revolutionary time: the division of revenue and expenditures into general state and local, and the hesitation on the part of some to include in the budget all the productive and distributive operations of the Supreme Council of National Economy and of the Commissariat for Food Supply. Both, the first and second obstacles have been somewhat surmounted, and the above-mentioned (third) revolutionary budget is already different from the two preceding budgets in many peculiarities which are very typical. These consist in a complete account of all production and distribution which the state has taken upon itself. This experiment is by no means complete, but the achievement should nevertheless be judged as considerable. The concrete conditions for making out the budget, as is stated in the explanatory note, have already made it possible to enter upon the road of accounting for the entire production and distribution of the nation, and that thereby the foundation has been laid down for the development of the budget in the only direction which is proper under the present conditions.

The budget of the first half of 1919 has followed the same fundamental principles for the construction of the state budget by including the expenditures of the entire state production and distribution as well as the sum total of the revenue-in the form of income from the productive and distributive operations of the state. In other words, this budget for the first time takes into account all the transactions of the Supreme Council of National Economy and of the Commissariat for Food Supply.

The further development of the budget will be directed toward the working out of the details of this general plan, and, in particular, toward differentiating revenue and expenditures: (1) direct, actual money received or paid, and (2) transactions involved in the accounting of material and labor, but not involving any actual receipts of money, or requiring any actual disbursements in money.

<h2 style="text-align:center">VI</h2>

In the field of taxation one must bear in mind first that the entire question of taxation has been radically changed with the beginning of Communist reconstruction.

Under the influence of the combined measures of economic and financial legislation of the Republic, the bases for the levying of land, real estate, industrial taxes, taxes on coupons, on bank notes, on stock, stock exchange, etc., completely disappeared, since the objects of taxation themselves have become government property. The old statute regulating the income tax (1916), which has not as yet been abolished, was in no way suitable to the changed economic conditions. All this compelled the Commissariat of Finance to seek new departures in the field of taxation.

However, it was impossible to give up the idea of direct taxation prior to the complete reformation of the tax system as a whole. Our work of Communist reconstruction has not been completed; it would be absurd to exempt from taxation the former capitalists as well as the newly forming group of people who strive for individual accumulation. This is why the system of direct taxation, which has until recently been in operation, was composed of fragments of the old tax on property and of the partly reformed income tax law. However, beginning with November, 1918, to this old system there were added two taxes of a purely revolutionary character which stand out apart within the partly outgrown system "taxes in kind" (decree of October 30, 1918) and "extraordinary taxes" (November 2, 1918).

Both decrees have been described as follows by Comrade Krestinsky, Commissary of Finance, at the May session of the financial sub-divisions:

"These are decrees of a different order, the only thing they have in common is that they both bear a class character and that each provides for the tax to increase in direction proportion with the amount of property which the tax-payer possesses, that the poor are completely free from both taxes, and the lower middle class pays them in a smaller proportion."

The extraordinary tax aims at the savings which remained in the hands of the urban and larger rural bourgeoisie from former times. Insofar as it is directed at non-labor savings it cannot be levied more than once. As regards the taxes in kind, borrowing Comrade Krestinsky's expression, "it will remain in force during the period of transition to the Communist order, until the village will from practical experience realize the advantage of rural economy on a large scale compared with the small farming estate, and will of its own accord, without compulsion, *en masse* adopt the Communist method of land cultivation."

Thus, the tax in kind is a link binding politically the Communist socialized urban economy and the independent individual petty agricultural producers.

Such are the two "direct" revolutionary taxes of the latest period. In regard to the old system of pre-revolutionary taxes, the work of the Commissariat of Finance during all of the latest period followed the path of gradual change and abolition of the already outgrown types of direct taxation and partial modification and adaptation to the new conditions of the moment, of the old taxes still suitable for practical purposes.

At the present moment the Commissariat of Finance has entered, in the domain of direct taxation reforms, upon the road toward a complete revolution in the old system. The central tax board is now, for the transitional period, working on a project of income and property taxation, the introduction of which will liquidate all the existing direct taxes, without exception. The single tax which is being proposed, is so constructed that it covers the very property of the citizen, i.e., it constitutes a demand that the citizen yield that part of his savings which is above a certain standard, etc.

In closing the review of the activity of the Commissariat of Finance during the two years of its existence, one must note briefly the great purely organizational work, conducted by it on a natural as well as a local scale.

The reform has been definitely directed towards simplifying the apparatus and reducing its personnel as far as possible.

Finally, with this reform, the Commissariat of Finance has been organized in the following manner: the central office, the central budget-accounting board (former People's Bank and Department of State Treasury) and, finally, the central tax board (former Department of Assessed Taxes and of Unassessed Taxes). Upon the same pattern are also being modeled the local financial bodies.

REPORTS: (A) METAL INDUSTRY; (B) DEVELOPMENT OF RURAL INDUSTRIES; (C) NATIONALIZATION OF AGRICULTURE

DOCUMENT IV — A, B, C

From *Economic Life*, (Nov. 7, 1919). The official organ
of the Supreme Council of National Economy
Finance, food, trade, and industry

A — OUR METAL INDUSTRY

The two years that have passed since the November Revolution have been marked by civil war, which still continues. Russia's isolation from the outside world, the loss and, later on, the recapture of entire provinces of decisive importance to her industries, the feverish, and therefore unsystematic, transfer of the industries to a peace basis, and then, during the last year the reorganization of the industries, the unusual conditions of transportation, the fuel and the food questions, and as a result of these, the question of labor power growing more acute—this is the sad picture of conditions under which the Russian proletariat has organized and maintained the nation's economic life.

And though these familiar conditions of actual life have affected all branches of industry, the greatest sufferer in this respect has been the metal industry, which forms the basis for our defence and the foundation for all our industrial life.

We might add here that the metal industry, and in particular the metal working industry as its most complicated and many-sided phase, both in assortment of products and in the nature of production, was by no means strong in Russia even under the rule of the bourgeoisie. As compared with the more developed capitalist countries, the metal industry in Russia has been at a disadvantage because of the very geographical situation of its centers, remote from the sources of raw material and fuel, artificially built up and having suffered all the consequences of an unsound foundation. As a result of these conditions, there is lack of specialization and poor development of large scale production which means a lack of the necessary prerequisites for successful production.

These are the external conditions under which the administration of our metal industry has been compelled to work.

The first and most fundamental problem has been that of systematic monopolization of industry. Only under this form of industrial organization—if freed from all the negative features of the capitalist trust,—is operation possible, even on a reduced scale, so that later on we might lay the solid foundations for new constructive work in the organization of the nation's economic life of Socialist principles. The process of monopolization may be considered as complete by this time. Large associations have been formed, such as the trust of united government machine shops "Gomza," amalgamating the largest mills producing the means of transportation and machine construction, and the large metallurgical mills, the trust of state copper working factories, the trust of government automobile works, the trust of government aviation work, the trust of government wire nail, bolt and nut factories, the trust of the Maltzoff Metallurgical mills, the association of the Kaluga metallurgical mills (cast iron, utensils, and hardware), the trust of the Podolsk mechanical and machine construction shops the Petrograd mills for heavy production, the Petrograd mills for medium machine construction, and the Petrograd mills for heavy output (production on large scale) are united under individual district administration boards.

Not all the enterprises consolidated within the associations have become closely bound up among themselves during this transitional period. In a matter of such gigantic proportions mistakes have been, of course, inevitable and they will have to be rectified. However, the results of the experience of the last two years are sufficient ground for the claim that the working class has solved the problem of consolidating industry.

The central administration of the Gomza mills thus characterizes the significance of this consolidation: "The consolidation of the mills working on transportation equipment, working with the metallurgical group makes it possible to utilize most efficiently all the resources available, such as fuel, raw material, technical forces, and the experience of the various mills with a view to obtaining the best possible results under the existing conditions. The amalgamation of the mills has already, during the past year, made it possible to distribute among them in the most rational manner, that inconsiderable quantity of metal products and mineral fuel, all products included, which the groups had in its possession. This enabled the mills to adapt themselves to the usage of local fuel. The concentration, even though only partial, of some of the branches of the metallurgical industry, also of the blacksmithing and iron foundry branches, was made possible entirely by the amalgamation. The specialization of the mills, according to the types of steam engines, Diesel or other machines, has been decided along general lines, by the Metal Department of the Supreme Council of National Economy, and the question is being worked out in closest cooperation with the Technical Department of the "Gomza." The amalgamation of the mills will make it possible to carry out gradually this specialization and utilize its results.

The central administration of the united mills states, in a report of its activities, that owing to the consolidation of the mills, the problems of supplying them with raw material, fuel and labor power, were solved in a fairly satisfactory way, thus placing production on a more or less constant basis. The mills entering this combination, if left to their own resources, would have been doomed to a complete shutdown.

The trust of the airplane building works has so completely amalgamated all the mills, which entered the combination that it now would be at a loss to determine in advance which of the mills would perform any given part of its program of production; to such an extent are these mills bound up together through constant interchange of fuel, raw material, supplies and even labor power.

The process of concentration of the industries in the Ural region is being successfully carried out by the Bureau of the Metal Department, through the organization of district and circuit officers.

Outside of the combine only those mills remained where production is merely organized: the Moscow works "Metal," "Electrosteel," "Scythe," "Aviation Outfits," and the Satatov mill—"Star" (Zwezda). These works are temporarily in the immediate charge of the Metal Department.

The Gomza trust during the entire period of its existence, up to July 1st, 1919, has produced 69 new locomotives and repaired 38 old ones; it has produced 1,744 new and repaired 1,040 old coaches; it has completed 670 small cars; 261,327 poods of axles and tires; 7,543 poods of switches; and 118,659 poods of various locomotive and car parts. The table given below representing the output for the first six months of 1919, as compared with the same period for 1916 and 1918, of the Vyxunsk Mining District, gives an idea of the work of the Department of Metallurgy of our largest trust:

	Output in Thousands of Poods				Ratio		
	I January to June, 1916	II January to June, 1918	III July to Dec., 1918	IV January to June, 1919	IV:I	IV:II	IV:III
Standard bars	86,7	91,4	74,2	133,6	154	146,1	179,9
Roofing iron and billets	...	...	37,3	37,3	...	..	100,0
Sheet iron and boiler plates	112,1	59,3	3,5	10,9	9,7	18,4	321,1
Plough shares and mould-boards	...	...	...	7,7	...	...	...
Pipes	225,4	125,0	56,4	61,1	24,7	78,8	108,2
Wire	255,2	106,7	4,9	22,6	8,8	21,2	455,1
Nails	114,9	117,4	79,3	51,4	44,8	43,8	64,9
Pitchforks	...	2,8	3,7	1,0	...	36,6	27,2
Shovels	6,6	6,0	4,5	2,2	33,7	37,3	50,5
	800,9	508,6	263,8	327,8	40,9%	64,5	124,2

It is apparent from the data given in the above table that the total output for the first six months of 1919 was almost 41 per cent of the total output for the corresponding period of 1916, and 64.5 per cent of the total product for the first half year of 1918, and 124.2 per cent of the last six months of 1918. The figures expressing the ratio of the total output of metal for the same periods are respectively—91.4 per cent, 120.6 per cent and 153.2 per cent.

Taking into consideration the extremely difficult conditions of production, the results may be considered satisfactory.

If we turn to the production of another of our trusts—"Central Copper Works" (Centromed), we note that during the period of October to December, 1916, the main Tula factory has produced 73.4 per cent of its capacity, during January to June of 1919—89.9 per cent, and finally during July and August of this year (1919)—about 87 per cent. The Kolchugin works have produced the various articles of their manufacture during the same periods in quantities which amounted to from 16 to 48 per cent, 30 per cent to 77 per cent and 20 per cent to 36 per cent of the quantities it was scheduled to produce, while the samovar factories have produced 44 per cent of the scheduled output.

The mills entering the association of the Central Aviation Works have produced 36 per cent to 180 per cent of the quantity they planned to turn out, while during July, August and September of 1918 this percentage ranged in the various mills and branches of production from 26 per cent to 120 per cent.

A comparatively considerable increase of production has been noted on the works combined in the automobile trust

It would be absolutely impossible, within the limits of a newspaper article, to amplify the illustration of the above statements by means of statistical data, especially in view of the fact that the data pertaining to the latest period has not been arranged systematically. However, the figures cited above, we trust, give some idea of the process and results of the concentration of industry and permit the deduction that the productivity of labor in our large works, insofar as it did not completely depend upon conditions which under the present circumstances are insuperable,—has increased as compared with that for the preceding year, and in some exceptional cases, it has even arisen to the pre-war level.

Nevertheless, our large industry has been getting into even greater difficulties. A number of crises weighing on it are breaking down its last forces. Of these the most acute and serious are the fuel and food crises, the latter demoralizing labor. This enforced comparative idleness has been thoroughly utilized during the revolutionary period, for the purpose of preparing for the time when the external conditions would permit our large industries to run at full speed.

In addition to the work of adapting our industry to modern conditions of production (altering the mills to suit them to the usage of wood fuel, by changing the construction of the furnaces and cupolas) the Technical Council of the Metals Department of the Supreme Council of National Economy is conducting the enormous work of standardizing the industry and specializing the mills by means of a detailed study of the individual branches of industry. It is also engaged in the restoration of the old, and in the organization of new, industries on the basis of specialized labor and production on a large scale. This latter task has been carried out by a number of commissions organized by the Metal Department of the Supreme Council of National Economy.

The Technical Council of the Metals Department conducted its work chiefly on the plane of standardizing production within the metal industry, reducing to a minimum the types of construction of the same article. Under capitalist conditions of production the law of competition frequently led individual manufacturers to deliberately flood the market with a multitude of various constructions of the same machines in order to compel the consumer purchasing a machine or implement at a given mill, to buy all the parts and often have his machine repaired in the same shop. It is needless to point out to what extent this increased the cost of production and, what is still more important, the cost of exploitation. The Technical Council has tackled the question not from an abstractly scientific viewpoint, but from a practical standpoint, working in close cooperation with our metal works. Every master part, every detail is being worked out on the basis of data collected at the mills by subcommittees consisting of specialists. Then the project is submitted to the mills where the necessary changes and coordination are suggested. The comments given by the mills are compiled and revised, before this or the other table or drawing is introduced; the same applies to the technical specifications and assortments.

Master parts of three categories are being worked out: (1) for the production of metal ware on a large scale, (2) for general machine construction, (3) for the construction of Diesel engines, which is now developing into a general division of thermo-technics.

In addition to this, a project is being completed for a lathe designed for the needs of home industries, and for repair work. A project is being worked out for a series of lathes of all sizes, required for machine construction shops.

Besides work on the standardization of industry, efforts are also being made to lay down the technical conditions.

Of the above mentioned committees, the following deserve special mention:

(1) The committee on steam turbine construction is distributing orders for the construction of turbines of various types. The Petrograd metal works and the Putiloff wharf have already completed part of their orders. In addition to this, the committee has investigated the construction of steam turbines in Russia.

(2) The committee on tractor construction has redistributed and again alloted orders among the Obukhov factory, the Mamin mill and the Kolomenksky mill for 75, 16 and 30 horse-power tractors. The drawings for the latter type of tractor have been worked out by the committee. Out of the number of tractors ordered at the Obukhov works, the first three Russian-made tractors are already completed. The others will be turned out in January and in June of 1920. It is proposed to organize the production of tractors on a large scale at the new Vyxunsk mill, the building of which is being completed.

(3) The committee on the construction of gas generating installations which has determined the basic type of gas generating engine most suitable for the conditions of Russian machine construction, has standardized the normal power of the engines; it has also outlined the preliminary measures for the adaptation of certain mills to large scale production of gas-generating engines.

(4) The committee for the development and improvement of steam boiler construction in Russia, has prepared the material and worked out detailed conditions for a contest of stationary water-tube boilers, the cheapest as to cost of production and the most economical in operation to be adopted by the committee. The committee also prepares the conditions for a contest on the production of a mechanical stoker, having investigated possible productivity and modern methods of production of steam boilers in Russia.

(5) The committee on the construction of refrigerating ma-

chinery ascertained the requirements for 1919–1920 in the line of refrigerating machinery; it is laying down and determining the types of refrigerating machines and apparatus that would be most desirable; it is working out the construction of the same, etc. Finally, it has drawn up plans for the construction of refrigerator-barges to sail regularly on the Volga between Astrakhan and Rybinsk.

In addition to the above-mentioned commissions, the Metal Department has a number of committees now functioning, such as the committee in charge of supplying the country with high grades of steel, having a technical convention of its own the committee on the organization of the Ural industries, the committee on locomotive construction, etc.

As we have mentioned before, simultaneously with rendering support to large industries and taking steps for their conversion to normal conditions, particularly careful attention had to be given to the intermediate, small and home industries.

Intermediate industry comprises almost all of the agricultural machine construction, under the direction of the agricultural machinery section of the Metal Department of the Supreme Council of National Economy. This section operates in close contact with the local governing bodies in charge of the people's industries: provincial, councils of national economy. According to the data of the section, covering the period of October 1st, 1918 to October 1st, 1919, the following simple as well as complicated agricultural machines and implements have been produced:

    147,453 ploughs
    3,717 winnowing machines
    1,440 straw cutters
    11,451 harrows
    98,689 scythes
    684,420 sickles
    11,980 harvesting machines

For the purpose of organizing the production of scythes in the most efficient manner possible the agricultural machine section created a special Scythes Bureau, which is investigating this line of production, ascertaining the possible amount of productivity if manufactured in the machine shop manner or according to the home industry method, both in the central provinces and in the Ural region. The bureau has laid down a plan for radical change in the nature of production by means of splitting it into two fundamental processes: the metallurgical—the rolling of steel of worked out profile; and the finishing process in the mills and shops. For the purpose of rolling the metal it has been proposed to utilize the Vyxunsk mill, which has been requested to include in its program the rolling of steel for the production of scythes.

In the field of home industry production on a small scale the committee on metal products and apparatus of the Metal Department is working in close cooperation with other government institutions, having organized agencies in Pavlovsk, Tula, Murom, and Vladimir, for the purpose of financing artisans and distributing raw material among them on the one condition that they turn in their product to the government stores for organized distribution. The results of this work can be judged by the following approximate data on the cost of manufactured products, the stock on hand from previous year returned to the factories and enterprises of the Murom, Pavlovsk, Tula region, as well as to the group of cast iron foundries of the provinces of Kaluga and Ryazan.

The Murom district, manufacturing cutlery and to some extent also instruments, has turned out, during the period following the organization of the government agency, 15 million roubles' worth of goods, while the total worth of it, including remnants returned, amounts to 25 million roubles; the Pavlovsk district engaged in the manufacture of cutlery, locks and instruments,—among others, surgical instruments—has produced since October 1st, 1918, 70 million roubles' worth of merchandise; including the remnants, this would aggregate to 100 million roubles. The Tula district (hardware, locks, stove accessories, samovars, hunters' rifles), has produced since May 1919, 30 million roubles' worth of goods, which, including the remnants, amount to 60 million roubles. The cast-iron foundries of the Kaluga and Ryazan districts (manufacturing cast-iron utensils, stove accessories and various other castings) have produced since October 1st, 1918, 50 million roubles' worth of merchandise, including the remnants.

Thus, the total amount of goods produced amounts to 165 million roubles,—or to 235 million roubles, if the value of the remnants is added,—taking 40 as the co-efficient of its value according to peace-time prices.

The central administration could not take upon itself the direct organization of home industries to the full extent. Its best assistants in this matter are the local institutions of national economy—the provincial and district metal committees, which have been brought in close contact with the central administration by the conventions of the representatives of the district and provincial metal committees. These conventions were being called at regular intervals for the purpose of working out and ratifying their programs concerning production and distribution of metals, and financial questions.

We must also mention the fact that all the measures in the domain of the metal industry are being carried out with the close and immediate cooperation of the workers' producing association—the union of metal workers.

Thus, as has been proven from practical experience, the methods and forms of organization of the metal industry have turned out to be correct. Their application is therefore to be continued and widened, strengthening the ties binding these organizations with the local administrative bodies, such as the provincial and district metal committees and with the central management of the amalgamated enterprises.

The great obstacle in the path of future development in our metal industry is the food question, which carries with it the dissolution of labor power. Considering the fact that circumstances have compelled our industry in general, and particularly the metal industry, to supply chiefly the needs of national defence, to which it is necessary to give right of way over all other interests, the authorities and the labor organizations must do everything in their power to avert the food crisis threatening the metal workers, even if this be to the detriment of the population.

It is necessary not only to cease all further mobilization of laborers and responsible workers, but also to select a considerable portion of those already mobilized for the purpose of transferring them from the army into industry.

The course of work of the metal industry during the past two years gives us reason to hope that these measures, if introduced systematically, might make it possible to cope with the difficult external conditions and furnish a mighty stimulus for preparing the metal industry for the needs of peaceful construction.

M. VINDELBOT.

THE DEVELOPMENT OF THE RURAL INDUSTRIES
B—FROM "ECONOMIC LIFE," Nov. 7, 1919.

The Supreme Council of National Economy has put into practice the idea of nationalization of all our industries: at present there is not one mill or factory of any considerable size that is not the property of the people.

During the second year of its existence, the Supreme Council of National Economy has made some headway in the work of nationalization of land. As a particular instance we might cite the fact that it was upon the initiative and due to the energetic efforts of the Supreme Council of National Economy that the land fund for the sugar industry has been nationalized. The total area of land nationalized for the sugar industry amounts to 600,000 dessiatins.

The sugar-beet industry has furnished the initial step in the development of the rural industries, since this particular industry has been better preserved during the transitional period of the Revolution. The alcohol industry occupies the next place. Its development has been begun by the Supreme Council of National Economy during the last few days.

These two large branches of rural industry are followed by a number of lesser significance, such as the production of starch, molasses, butter, milk, tobacco, medicinal herbs, the group of fibre plants, etc. The Supreme Council of National Economy is now laying a solid foundation for the development of all these industries.

What then is the program of action of the Supreme Council of National Economy for the development of the rural industries? In the first place, to supply definite land areas for the cultivation of certain plants, the introduction of definite forms of agricultural labor, and of uniform management for the manufacturing and agricultural industries, the establishment of close connections between the industrial proletariat and the citizens engaged in the rural industries.

Among the problems enumerated above, foremost is that of uniting the industrial proletariat with the rural workers. The Supreme Council of National Economy has already begun to work on this task. Thus the industrial proletariat is now officially in possession of 90,000 dessiatins of land, on which communes have been organized. The crops from these estates go to satisfy the needs of the associations in whose name the estates are registered. At the same time, the industrial proletariat, through participation in agricultural labor, is introducing new ideas into the rural industries.

The Supreme Council of National Economy is mining the coal from the depths of the earth and exploiting the peat deposits. In order to utilize the resources completely, it is paying particular attention to the conversion of swampy areas and exhausted turf deposits into areable land, transforming the bottom of the exploited turf areas into vegetable gardens, the sections bordering upon the swamps into artificial meadows, and the uplands into fields. During last summer similar work was accomplished on a considerable scale on the lands of the central electric station, in the Government of Moscow, the Ilatur electric station, in the Government of Ryazan, Gus-Hrustalny, in the Government of Vladimir, and the Gomza estates in the Government of Nizhni-Novgorod. Thus, during last summer, the work was organized in four central provinces, abounding in large areas of land, which cannot be conveniently used for agricultural purposes.

Simultaneously the improvement of dwellings, and the building of garden-cities is being given careful and immediate consideration. This work is being carried on by the Supreme Council of National Economy at the electric station of Kashirsk, the Shatur station and the Central Electric station.

In order to unify rural industries the Supreme Council of National Economy has formed the central administration of agricultural estates and industrial enterprises, assigning to it the task of uniting and developing as far as possible, the work of the rural mills.

The Central Administration of Agriculture considers it one of its immediate problems to propagate widely the idea of nationalization of land for all rural industries and the opening of new districts for those industries.

In apportioning the land, especially valuable districts should be set apart, such as the meadows, flooded with water from the Don river, fully suitable for the cultivation of tobacco, fibre plants, and olives, on a large scale.

These lands, if distributed among the peasants will never yield such wealth as they could do were they nationalized for rational exploitation.

Next on the program of the Central Administration of Agriculture is the building up of new branches of rural industry, such as the working of sugar beets into molasses and into beet flour, in the northern districts, the production of ammonium sulphate out of the lower grades of peat, the preparation of fodder out of animal refuse, the production of turf litter material, the preparation of new sources of nitrate fertilizer out of peat, etc.

Electric power must be utilized for the cultivation of land. The practical realization of this problem has been started on the fields of the electric power transmission department. This Fall we succeeded in tilling the ground by means of a power-driven plow.

In order to build up the rural industries, practical work must be carried on, simultaneously with that which is being done on the particularly important lands, also on such lands as will not be the bone of contention between the proletariat and the peasantry.

What lands are these? The swampy areas, the forest-covered lands, those districts where the people are starving, the dry lands, the scarcely populated districts, etc.

These are the brief outlines of the program. The foundations of absolutely all of the development of rural industry mentioned have been laid down. The practical steps for the materialization of the plans have to some extent already been, or are being, undertaken.

All of this work the Supreme Council of National Economy had to carry out under extremely difficult conditions. Prior to that, a considerable part of the sources of raw material for the rural industries has been completely torn away from the Soviet Republic. Another serious hindrance was the insufficient number of already existing organizations, which would be capable of fulfilling the tasks outlined by the Council. A considerable amount of harm has been done to this work by inter-departmental friction.

But difficult as the present conditions may be, and no matter how strong is the desire of the former ruling classes to turn back the tide of life, this is impossible and can never take place.

CENTRAL ADMINISTRATION OF AGRICULTURE.

NATIONALIZATION OF AGRICULTURE
C—FROM "ECONOMIC LIFE," Nov. 7, 1919.

The nationalization of agriculture is one of the most complicated problems of the Socialist Revolution, and perhaps in no other country is this problem as complex as in Soviet Russia.

At the time when the decree on Socialist land management was made public, the fundamental elements of nationalization had hardly begun to take shape: the territory affected by nationalization was by no means defined; there was not the personnel necessary for the creation and enforcement of any plan concerning production; the large masses of laborers hardly understood the idea of nationalization and in some instances were hostile to the measures by means of which the Soviet power was carrying out the program of nationalization.

In order to summarize the results of the work, which began on a nation-wide scale in March, 1919, and to estimate these results, one must first realize the conditions which formed the starting-point for the work of the People's Commissariat of Agriculture at the time when it commenced to carry out the nationalization of agriculture.

The extent of the capitalist heritage, which our organized Soviet estates now have at their disposal, amounts to 615,503 dessiatins or areable land, situated in the Soviet provinces and formerly in the hands of private owners. Eighty-five per cent of the areable land, which formerly belonged to the landed aristocracy was taken over for the purpose of both organized and non-organized distribution—chiefly the latter.

The equipment of the various estates was diminished and destroyed to no lesser extent. Instead of the 386,672 privately owned horses, registered in the Soviet provinces, according to the census of 1916, the Soviet estates in the hands of the People's Commissariat of Agriculture received 23,149 horses—a number hardly sufficient for the cultivation of one-third of the area under cultivation now belonging to the Soviet estates. Of the 290,969 cows—only 43,361 came into the possession of the Soviet estates. The entire number of horses and cows will yield sufficient fertilizer for only 13,000 dessiatins of fallow land, i.e., about 10 per cent of the area intended to be converted into areable land.

The supply of agricultural machinery and implements was in the same condition.

The Soviet estates had almost no stocks of provisions. The workmen were compelled either to steal or to desert for places where bread was more abundant.

The winter corn was sowed in the fall of 1918 on very limited areas (not over 25 per cent of the fallow land), very often without fertilizer, with a very small quantity of seeds to each dessiatin. In 13 out of 36 Soviet provinces (governments) no winter corn has been sowed at all.

A considerable portion of the estates taken over by the People's Commissariat of Agriculture could not be utilized due to the lack of various accessories, such as harness, horseshoes, rope, small instruments, etc.

The workers were fluctuating, entirely unorganized, politically inert—due to the shortage of provisioning and of organization. The technical forces could not get used to the village; besides, we did not have sufficient numbers of agricultural experts familiar with the practical organization of large estates. The regulations governing the social management of land charged the representatives of the industrial proletariat with a leading part in the work of the Soviet estates. But torn between meeting the various requirements of the Republic of prime importance, the proletariat could not with sufficient speed furnish the number of organizers necessary for agricultural management.

The idea of centralized management on the Soviet estates has not been properly understood by the local authorities, and the work of organization from the very beginning had to progress amidst bitter fighting between the provincial Soviet estates and the provincial offices of the Department of Agriculture. This struggle has not yet ceased.

Thus, the work of nationalizing the country's agriculture began in the spring, i.e., a half year later than it should have, and without any definite territory (every inch of it had to be taken after a long and strenuous siege on the part of the surrounding population), with insufficient and semi-ruined equipment, without provisions, without an apparatus for organization and without the necessary experience for such work, with the agricultural workers engaged in the Soviet estates having no organization at all.

According to our preliminary calculations, we are to gather in the Fall of this year a crop of produce totaling in the 2,524 Soviet estates as follows:

	Poods	Area in Dessiatins
Winter crop	1,798,711	54,000
Spring corn	4,765,790	97,720
Potatoes	16,754,900	23,754
Vegetables, approximately	4,500,000	4,659

Of the Winter corn we received only a little over what was required for seed (in a number of provinces the crops are insufficient for the consumption of the workers of the Soviet estates).

The Soviet estates are almost everywhere sufficiently supplied with seeds for the spring crops.

The number of horses used on the Soviet estates has been increased through the additional purchase of 12,000 to 15,000.

The number of cattle has also been somewhat increased.

The Soviet estates are almost completely supplied with agricultural implements and accessories, both by having procured new outfits from the People's Commissariat for Provisioning and by means of energetic repair work on the old ones.

The foundation has been laid (in one-half of the provinces sufficiently stable foundations) for the formation of an organizational machinery for the administration of the Soviet estates.

Within the limits of the Soviet estates the labor union of the agricultural proletariat has developed into a large organization.

In a number of provinces the leading part in the work of the Soviet estates has been practically assumed by the industrial proletariat, which has furnished a number of organizers, whose reputation had been sufficiently established.

Estimating the results of the work accomplished, we must admit that we have not as yet any fully nationalized rural economy. But during the eight months of work in this direction, all the elements for its organization have been accumulated.

We have strengthened our position in regard to supplies, having been enabled not only to equip more efficiently the Soviet estates (2,524) already included in our system of organization, but also to nationalize during the season of 1920 additional 1,012 Soviet estates, with an area of 972,674 dessiatins. The combined area of the nationalized enterprises will probably amount in 1920 to about 2,000,000 dessiatins within the present Soviet territory.

A preliminary familiarity with individual estates and with agricultural regions makes it possible to begin the preparation of a national plan for production on the Soviet estates and for a systematic attempt to meet the manifold demands made on the nationalized estates by the agricultural industries: sugar, distilling, chemical, as well as by the country's need for stock breeding, seeds, planting and other raw materials.

The greatest difficulties arise in the creation of the machinery of organization. The shortage of agricultural experts is being replenished with great difficulty, for the position of the technical personnel of the Soviet estates, due to their weak political organization, is extremely unstable. The mobilization of the proletarian forces for work in the Soviet estates gives us ground to believe that in this respect the spring of 1920 will find us sufficiently prepared.

The ranks of proletarian workers in the Soviet estates are drawing together. True, the level of their enlightenment is by no means high, but "in union there is strength" and this force, if properly utilized, will yield rapidly positive results.

In order to complete the picture of the agricultural work for the past year we are citing the following figures: the total expenditures incurred on the Soviet estates and on account of their administration up to January 1st, 1920, is estimated to amount to 924,347,500 roubles. The income, if the products of the Soviet estates are considered at firm prices, amounts to 843,372,343 roubles.

Thus, the first, the most difficult year, has ended without a deficit, if one excludes a part of the liabilities which are to be met during a number of years, i.e., horses and implements.

Of course, it is not the particular experience which the workers possess that has caused the favorable balance of the Soviet estates, this being mainly due to the fact that the productive work in the realm of agriculture under modern conditions is a business not liable to lose.

And this is natural: industry in all its forms depends upon the supply of fuel, raw material, and food. Nationalized rural economy has an inexhaustible supply of solar energy—a fuel supply independent of transportation of the blockade.

The fundamental element of production—land—does not demand any "colonial" means of restoration of its productivity. And as for provisions, these we get from the earth under the sun!

After eight months of work on the nationalization of our rural economy, as a result of two years of titanic struggle on the part of the proletariat for the right to organize the Socialist industries with its own hands,—is it not high time to admit that the most expedient, most far-sighted, and correct method to stabilize the Soviet power would be to use the greatest number of organized proletarian forces for the work of nationalizing our agriculture?

N. BOGDANOV.

Lector House believes that a society develops through a two-fold approach of continuous learning and adaptation, which is derived from the study of classic literary works spread across the historic timeline of literature records. Therefore, we aim at reviving, repairing and redeveloping all those inaccessible or damaged but historically as well as culturally important literature across subjects so that the future generations may have an opportunity to study and learn from past works to embark upon a journey of creating a better future.

This book is a result of an effort made by Lector House towards making a contribution to the preservation and repair of original ancient works which might hold historical significance to the approach of continuous learning across subjects.

HAPPY READING & LEARNING!

LECTOR HOUSE LLP
E-MAIL: lectorpublishing@gmail.com